NORTH CAROLINA
STATE BOARD OF COMMUNITY COLLEGES
LIBRARIES
CAPE FEAR TECHNICAL INSTITUTE

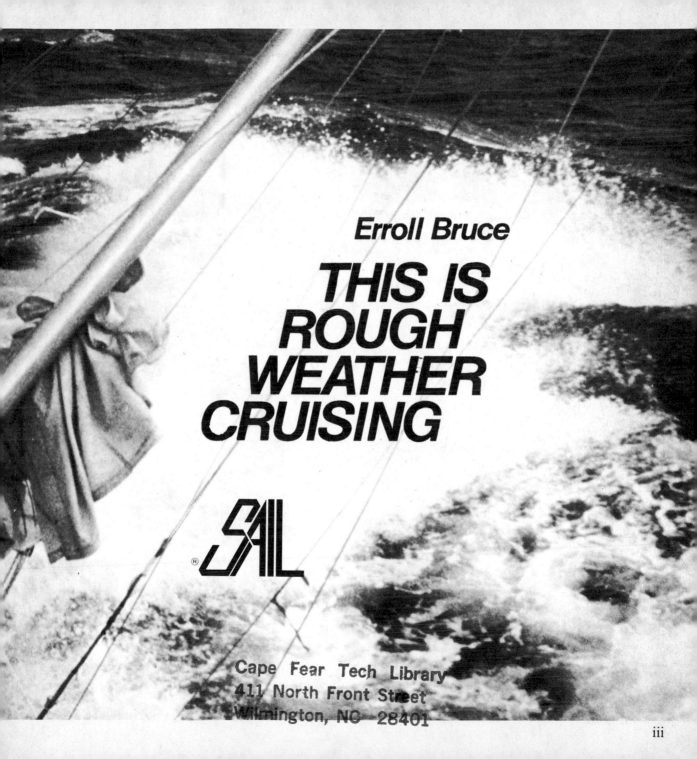

Erroll Bruce

THIS IS ROUGH WEATHER CRUISING

SAIL®

Cape Fear Tech Library
411 North Front Street
Wilmington, NC 28401

First published © 1980
by
United Nautical Publishers SA, Basle

First published in United States 1980
by
SAIL BOOKS, INC.
38 Commercial Wharf
Boston, Massachusetts

ISBN 0-914814-23-0

No part of this book or its
illustrations may be reproduced
without the permission of the Publishers.

Distributed to bookstores by
W. W. Norton & Company, Inc.

Text setting by: BAS Printers Limited, Over Wallop, England
Printing by: Grafiche Editoriali Padane, Cremona - Italy

Preface

This book aims to assist those who cruise their boats mainly in coastal waters the world over, and who appreciate that they might sometimes have to meet bad weather.

It is assumed that often such a boat will have on board a crew whose experience of the sea is modest; it might, for example, be two adults and a child or two. Frequently such a crew will include women, girls and boys; so the word 'man' in this book refers more to the species than the gender or state of maturity.

Man evolved as a land creature, so cannot rely upon instinctive guidance when going afloat. For instance, in a gale at sea the intuitive impulse of the landsman is to make for the nearest land, yet the experience of seamen shows that often it is much safer to stay out at sea.

We go to sea expecting a spice of danger; if we wanted only snug comfort and maximum safety we would have stayed on the land for which nature fitted us. In rough weather the thrill of adventure peaks; aboard a sound craft with a capable crew, we can actually enjoy a gale.

We have a 'front row seat' to a stirring display of nature's strength. It is a strength that can certainly destroy our puny little craft if we ignore the maxims of sound seamanship; but it need bring no unreasonable danger if we apply the lessons learned by generations of seafarers around the world who dared afloat before us.

This book is planned to give practical assistance to the skipper and his crew in the sequence in which problems come to them. The concentric method is used, with ideas developed as they apply to the particular stage; thus one subject may be mentioned several times as it crops up in varying ways at different stages of rough weather preparation and handling.

Acknowledgements

There are many who have contributed with their help, knowledge, special expertise and advice in the creation and preparation of this book.

First I thank my wife for her tolerance in cruising with me in small craft, sometimes when the problems of rough weather on deck were difficult to compromise with the claims of very small children down below.

In writing this book I have been greatly helped by working with men of the Royal National Lifeboat Institution to whom I am deeply indebted for showing me their sheer seamanship skill; by the late lifeboat Coxwain Harold Hayles, who allowed me the use of some of his dramatic photos; by the crews who came with me on four great sailing races across the North Atlantic Ocean and who mutually discovered with me how best we could understand the sea; by my children and grandchildren, besides hundreds of other young people who have cruised with me, some of whom may have thought I was teaching them!

Adlard Coles, my long time friend and rival afloat, has written a Foreword to this book. He has also contributed over the years countless hours of discussion and experiment in the handling of small craft in rough weather. I thank him most profoundly for his continual encouragement and support.

In the production of the book itself I am indebted to my publishing colleagues Konrad Wilhelm Delius, Dr. Silvio Mursia and Wim de Bruijn. Also to Richard Creagh-Osborne for preparing the layouts and general advice besides the photographs he took at sea. The brilliant artists who interpreted my often demanding ideas are to be congratulated on their remarkable achievements. They were Richard Everitt and Peter A. G. Milne.

Finally I acknowledge with grateful thanks all the photographers as listed below. If I have missed anyone I must give my apologies:

Daniel Forster, Switzerland—cover, 2.10, 3.1, 5.3, 6.1, 8.2
Harold Hayles, Yarmouth—1.23, 9.16, 11.1
H. J. Pinn, Bridport—8.8
Mike Peyton, Fambridge—Frontispiece, 3.8
Revue Bateaux, Paris—1.20, 4.1
Yacht Photo Service, Hamburg—1.18, 2.6
Richard Creagh-Osborne, Lymington—3.2, 3.4, 3.12, 3.18, 3.24, 4.7, 5.4, 5.6, 5.7, 6.7, 6.8, 6.9, 6.10, 7.1, 7.3, 7.6, 7.12, 7.14, 10.1, 11.9, 11.10

David Alan Williams—2.11
West Australian Newspapers—3.33, 3.34
Sarah King, London—6.2
James Novak, USA—9.7
Ian Tew, Lymington—2.2
Folkebadcentralen, Denmark—9.3
Van der Meulen, Holland—2.3
Practical Boat Owner—5.1
Jonathan Eastland, Portsmouth—7.5

Contents

Foreword

It is a privilege to have been invited to contribute an introduction to this book, and it is also a pleasure.

Let me explain that I first met Erroll Bruce in 1950, when we were rivals in the first official R.O.R.C. transatlantic race open to small boats. It was his experience in this event, and in the extra-tropical cyclone in which the boats were caught out in the earlier passage from Bermuda to Newport R.I., that led him to write his classic *Deep Sea Sailing*, first published in 1953. This book was so well received that it in turn led to the present work on rough sea sailing to help those in different parts of the world who cruise mainly in coastal waters. In some respects the latter subject is the more difficult since it is not until the mariner leaves the ocean astern and comes on soundings and narrow seas that he meets the land risks of lee shores, shoals, rocks and the strong tidal streams that cause dangerous races.

Commander Erroll Bruce has exceptional and diverse qualifications for his task. A former sub-mariner he later became a training officer and responsibility is a characteristic of his work. As a crewman in the Orkney lifeboat he saw seas at their worst in the notorious Pentland Firth. Subsequently he visited many lifeboat stations learning at first hand from the coxswains the reasons why so many yachts have got into difficulties and how these so often could have been avoided. Finally it may be added that as a family man himself he is familiar with the joys and responsibilities of family cruising with children.

As to the book itself its purpose is given in the preface 'To assist those who cruise their boats mainly in coastal waters the world over', and the remarkably comprehensive scope of his work is revealed in the detailed list of the contents and the illustrations linked with the text. One cardinal principle of the author is preparation in harbour, where everything should be checked and stowed under easy conditions and not left until the arrival of rough water. This could include practice with donning safety harness, which is often a tiresome and sick-making task if left to the last moment. To this subject of seasickness Erroll Bruce devotes considerable attention because it can be a major factor affecting the safety of small craft. *Mal de mer* ranges from mild discomfort involving disinclination to make effort to complete disability to do anything at all. Another matter on which the author writes firmly is that of excess speed adding to sailing risks, but with the proviso so often overlooked, that over-reefing can be equally dangerous if it leaves the boat so slow as to be at the mercy of strong tidal streams and lee shores.

Space limitations forbid further comment on the many original and practical features of the contents except to add that the final chapter 'When help is needed' shows Erroll Bruce at his best in the clarity with which he summarises the essential things which have to be done. The chapter is typical of them all, sharply focused on its subject, refusing embroidery and the temptation to add 'ifs and buts' which might confuse the reader.

I will finish this introduction on a personal note. I have enjoyed reading this thought provoking book. Indeed, although written for yachtsmen of relatively modest experience, it provides something of a refresher course for old hands at the game. *Rough Weather Cruising* is one of the most brilliantly conceived textbooks I have ever read. It will succeed in its object in helping to keep yachtsmen out of trouble now and for generations to come.

ADLARD COLES

Frontispiece. A cruising yacht weighs anchor for a night passage. But what will the weather bring? Is the yacht and her crew fully prepared?

1 Wind and sea

Wind

Wind is made up of a series of gusts and lulls, unlike the steady flow of air coming from a large fan. These gusts vary in strength and direction so that, although there may be a general wind direction, such as south-west, and a mean wind velocity, such as fifteen knots, a boat actually experiences quick changing forces which not only alter in strength and direction but also in the vertical plane.

The speed and progress of a sailing craft will depend mainly on the mean wind, but the strain on her gear and the chances of being knocked down or suffering other accidents depend just as much on the turbulence of the wind.

For instance a wind may blow steadily, gusting to twenty two knots and easing to eighteen, giving a mean wind speed of twenty. Yet this same mean speed could also be a blustery blow with squalls hurtling down from high cliffs at thirty five knots between lulls of no more than five. A boat would then not only be buffeted by a much higher top wind speed, but she would be subjected to the strain of rapid changes, just as a series of hammer blows will drive

10

in a nail much further than a steady pressure equal to the average force.

In general the stronger the mean wind force the greater is the turbulence, but apart from the lie of the land, such as hills to windward, turbulence will be affected by the particular meteorological conditions causing the wind. For instance the tropical maritime air which prevails over the oceans in moderate latitudes brings winds that are steady in strength and direction of which the best examples are the trade winds. Continental polar air, which abounds over the higher latitude land masses, is more turbulent.

Where air masses meet is called a front, and this always creates disturbed conditions. Especially is this so when a cold front passes over, with the cold polar air forcing its way under a mass of warm air. Then the wind veers suddenly to the north-west in the northern hemisphere, or backs to the south-west in the southern hemisphere. But in both hemispheres it becomes more turbulent and squally, although the barometer has begun to rise and the mean wind speed may actually have eased.

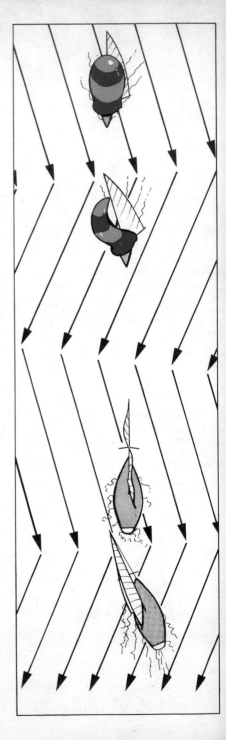

1.1 Winds vary in the horizontal plane (direction) to a greater or lesser extent. In strong winds the helmsman needs to watch carefully and adjust his course to avoid an accidental gybe, a knock-down, or an involuntary tack.

1.2 Also in the horizontal plane, winds vary in strength. Sometimes the variation is very marked (gusting), while in other types of weather it is gentle and scarcely noticeable.

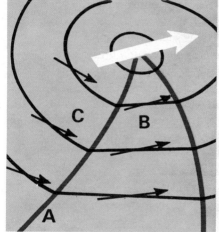

1.3 Wind coming off high ground is particularly turbulent. Certain weather conditions also produce winds that are turbulent both in the horizontal and vertical planes.

1.4 In a typical passing depression (nor- ▷ thern hemisphere) the passage of the cold front (A) causes a change in weather from reasonably steady winds and rain at B, to squally winds with clearing skies and showers at C.

Wind force (Beaufort Scale)

Beaufort Force	Wind speed in knots	Description of wind	Sea equivalent in open ocean
0	Less than	**Calm**	Sea like a mirror.
1	1—3	**Light air**	Ripples with the appearance of scales are formed but without foam crests.
2	4—6	**Light breeze**	Small wavelets, still short but more pronounced. Crests have a glassy appearance and do not break.
3	7—10	**Gentle breeze**	Large wavelets. Crests begin to break. Foam of glassy appearance. Perhaps scattered white horses.
4	11—16	**Moderate breeze**	Small waves, becoming longer: fairly frequent white horses.
5	17—21	**Fresh breeze**	Moderate waves, taking a more pronounced long form; many white horses are formed. (Chance of some spray.)
6	22—27	**Strong breeze**	Large waves begin to form; the white foam crests are more extensive everywhere. (Probably some spray.)
7	28—33	**Near gale**	Sea heaps up and white foam from breaking waves begins to be blown in streaks along the direction of the wind.
8	34—40	**Gale**	Moderately high waves of greater length; edges of crests begin to break into spindrift. The foam is blown in well-marked streaks along the direction of the wind.
9	41—47	**Strong gale**	High waves. Dense streaks of foam along the direction of the wind. Crests of waves begin to topple, tumble and roll over. Spray may affect visibility.
10	48—55	**Storm**	Very high waves with long overhanging crests. The resulting foam in great patches is blown in dense white streaks along the direction of the wind. On the whole the surface of the sea takes a white appearance. The tumbling of the sea becomes heavy and shocklike. Visibility affected.
11	56—63	**Violent storm**	Exceptionally high waves. (Small and medium-sized ships might be for a time lost to view behind the waves.) The sea is completely covered with long white patches of foam lying along the direction of the wind. Everywhere the edges of the wave crests are blown into froth. Visibility affected.
12	64—71	**Hurricane**	The air is filled with foam and spray. Sea completely white with driving spray; visibility very seriously affected.

a

b

c

Wind classification

The force of the wind is described in the Beaufort scale in many countries, and its direction is given as the point from which it blows. Thus a knowledge of the Beaufort scale is important as it is part of the language of weather forecasts. However it was devised for large sailing vessels and therefore needs careful interpretation when applied to small craft. Its figures refer to *average* wind velocity, while the small sailing craft is more affected by *peak* velocities and by turbulence.

Most people over-estimate the actual wind force when at sea, and hence a forecast for force 6, say, may be treated lightly. In addition, since it is an average speed, the gusts which will have to be faced may reach speeds well into the next force category, or higher.

As an actual example the tracing *(1.6)* from an anemometer shows how a wind of force 5 at 1500 on September 9 increased to force 6 by 1600 with a mean wind velocity of twenty five knots. However several gusts reached between thirty five and thirty seven knots, while some lulls dropped the wind speed to between ten and twelve knots.

The tracing in *1.7* also gives the wind direction at the same times and shows that while the mean direction at 1600 was 305 degrees, or around NW, actual gusts varied between 260 and 340 degrees.

1.5 a) Force 3 is a full-sail breeze which is unlikely to give wet decks.

b) Force 5 will need a reefed mainsail and a reduced headsail.

c) Force 8 is tough going! If still at sea, the yacht will only carry a small jib and fully reefed mainsail.

1.6 A tracing of a wind of force 5 increasing around 1600 to force 6.

1.7 A tracing of the actual direction of the same wind.

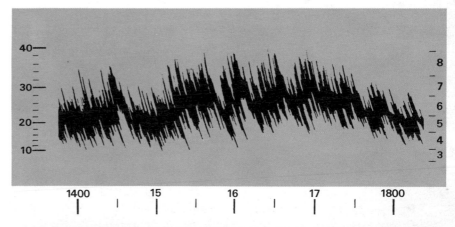

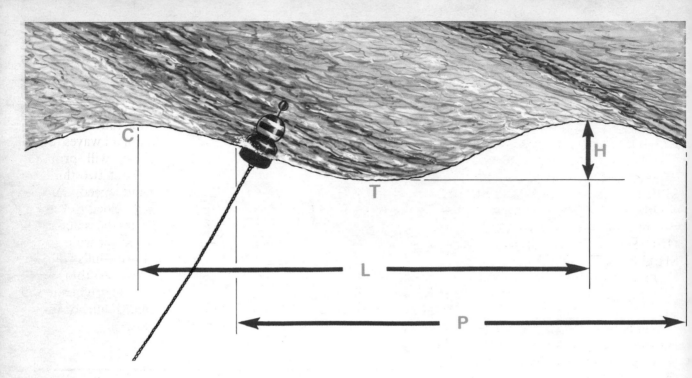

1.8 The theoretical wave is sine shaped. **L** is the length; **H**, the height; **C**, the crest; **T**, the trough; **P**, the period in seconds which is the time the wave takes to pass a given point.

1.9 The 'fetch' (**f**) is the open water distance over which the wind is blowing. The maximum possible wave height (**H**) for that wind force depends on the fetch.

Waves

A simple wave, caused solely by a steady wind, has five characteristics:

LENGTH—from one crest to the next.

PERIOD—the time taken for successive crests to pass a fixed point, such as a buoy.

SPEED—the velocity of a crest, although the water of which it is formed scarcely moves.

HEIGHT—from trough to crest.

SHAPE—approximates to a sine curve until the wind becomes strong.

Winds of a particular strength cause waves of a specific length which grow in height according to the time that that wind blows, up to an optimum height. The height also depends on the fetch, or length of sea over which that wind is blowing. For example, land fifty miles to windward will limit the average wave height to about two and a half metres in a gale of force 8, however long it blows.

The perfect wave only appears at sea in the form of a low swell coming from an area of high winds into an area of near calms. Such swell waves may run on for hundreds of miles in a deep ocean, maintaining their length, speed and period, but gradually losing height as they travel.

We saw earlier that the wind actually consists of a series of gusts and lulls, varying in strength and direction. Each of these contributes to a different wave pattern, and in a moderate gale the top gusts of perhaps forty knots may create waves which will travel at almost the speed of these gusts, but they will be low waves as such strong gusts only blow for a fraction of the time.

The predominant waves, which are the highest, will probably work up to about two-thirds of the mean wind speed, and so would reach a velocity of about twenty knots in the same near-gale. Then the lower wind speeds in the comparative lulls will produce slower waves, but again these will be low in height and will have only small influence on the overall sea pattern.

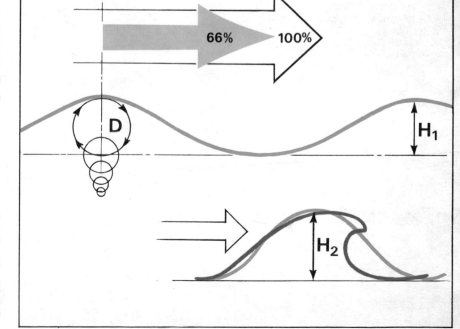

1.10 A drop of water (**D**) within a wave travels a roughly circular path, only moving forwards slightly in practice owing to wind friction near the surface. Wave speed in open water reaches around two thirds the prevailing wind speed. Wave height (**H**) is controlled by wind speed and water depth. When it becomes too steep (**H₂**) the crest collapses forwards under wind pressure.

Confused seas

These waves of differing heights will combine to form an irregular pattern, but there will also be waves arriving from differing angles caused by gusts and other influences. So a rough sea is a whole medley of different wave formations in which sometimes one wave will ride up on another to form an extra high crest— perhaps as much as 1.4 times the height of the individual higher waves.

With a wind change, such as often happens in a gale when a front passes, the mixture becomes even more chaotic as a new system of waves fights for domination. In this battleground two big waves will often buffet together expending much of their energy in a flurry of spray and foam. Yet occasionally these waves may synchronise and join forces to build a giant wave of almost their combined height.

Size of waves

From the cockpit of a small craft the wave length is often underestimated while the height is usually exaggerated. This matters chiefly in that someone who estimates that he has experienced a blow with seven metre waves, but which really had a mean height of three metres with four metres maximum, will find himself badly misled if he expects something less than the previous blow on hearing a forecast for six metre waves as this could even include the odd eight metre monster.

In the open sea a properly prepared yacht, even if she is small, should have no fear of a force 8 gale. In the summer months in temperate zones, avoiding any areas which might be affected by tropical storms, full gales seldom last for more than six hours, and in that time the mean wave height in the open sea, when little influenced by current or tidal streams, should scarcely get above three metres.

This is still quite a high wave, but the normal length would be nearly one hundred metres so the gradient of the wave face up which the craft must climb should be no problem unless the boat's own speed makes her plunge hard into it.

Should the wind shift appreciably, say 30 degrees or more as the weather front passes over, and the strength remain the same, then the higher waves will mount up to some five metres or more, but within an hour the new system will be established and the seas will settle to a more modest and regular pattern.

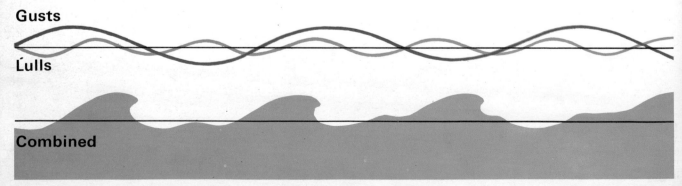

Gusts

Lulls

Combined

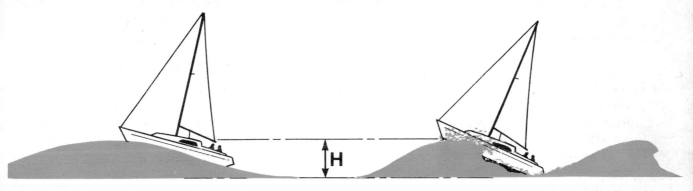

Wave gradient

It is not the height of a wave which endangers a yacht so much as its gradient. The smallest boat will happily rise to a six metre wave if it is two hundred metres long. Yet the same boat could be knocked about by a two metre wave if it is short and has a breaking top.

As the wind rises the rate of increase in wave height is greater than the rate of increase in length; so the waves get steeper. In open water this steepness reaches a limit beyond which energy from the wind is dissipated by the waves breaking or foaming at the crest. As these waves break they reach their greatest gradient.

1.12 It is the wave's steepness rather than its height which affects a yacht. If it is also breaking or the yacht's speed is high the effect will be greater still.

1.13 From the low position of a yacht's cockpit in the trough it is easy to over-estimate the height of the approaching crest.

1.11 The waves induced by gusts and lulls are of differing sizes and directions. They combine to form a confused pattern on the surface with some waves of a greater height than any one individual wave.

Effects of currents and tidal streams

Currents and tidal streams, and also changes in the depth of the sea, have an important influence on wave gradient too.

On the turn of the tide the current may become contrary; the waves then gain height and lose length, thus becoming steeper. More will therefore break if they are already near their maximum gradient. However, if waves travel into a stream running in the same direction as themselves they in- crease in length and lose height, thus becoming easier for a boat to negotiate.

Horizontal movement of water may be caused by a current, such as the flow of river water from its source until well out to sea, or an ocean current caused by prevail- ing winds, or even by a flow of water replacing that evaporated in a hot, enclosed sea such as the Mediterranean. The flow will de- pend on the amount of rain in the catchment area, the vigor of the prevailing wind or the rate of evaporation, but in general all these currents are permanent or semi-permanent movements of water, unlike tidal currents which change direction every few hours.

Currents tend to be speeded up and diverted in direction when restricted, such as through the Strait of Messina between Italy and Sicily, or when the flow is channelled between shoals in an

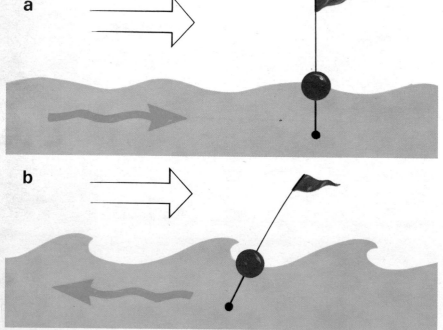

a

b

1.14 *Wind with current* means smoother more rounded waves. Wind speed over a free floating object is true wind *less* current speed (**a**).

Wind against current means steeper more peaked waves, probably with breaking crests. A free floating object feels the true wind plus the current speed (**b**).

1.15 Permanent currents are caused by prevailing wind, out-flow from large rivers (**A**), replacement of evaporation (**B**). Currents fan into and out of re- stricted zones (**C**) and strengthen in the narrowest parts or round headlands (**D**).

estuary, or where the warm current has to force its way between a coastline and a mass of colder water.

Horizontal movement of water due to tides is caused by the rise and fall. As the tide normally rises for about six hours the tidal stream in an estuary will flow inwards and then turn seawards for the next six hours. However, heavy rain inland will affect the resulting movement, perhaps halting the inwards flowing flood stream altogether, but giving extra strength to the outward ebb flow.

Near coasts the tidal stream will be changed by the shape of the land and the shoals, in some places becoming rotary and setting in a different direction each hour; in practically all cases the tidal streams change at least every few hours.

Whatever the cause of this horizontal movement it can have a major effect on the character of the seas even in deep water; but it is important for the seaman to know whether this is due to current, which will persist for a matter of days or even months, or whether it is tidal stream, which will probably change soon. Note that even in mid-ocean a current may have a clear-cut boundary.

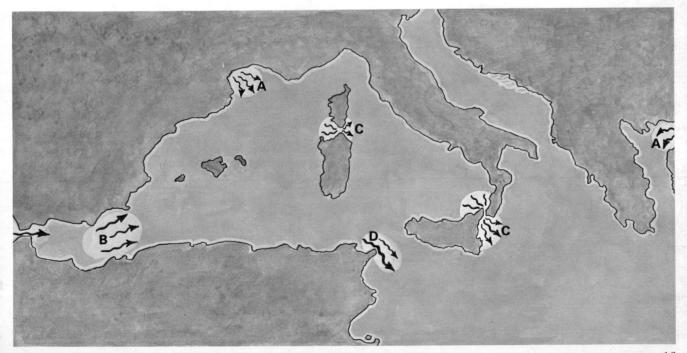

Shallow water effects

When deep water waves move into gradually shoaling water, their character begins to be affected when the depth is less than half the wave length. Thus, for example, a fresh north-wester blowing across the North Sea would, after twelve hours, create a sea in the Heligoland Bight with two metre high average waves, having a period of about eight seconds and a length of some eighty metres. This means that the shallow water effects begin in depths of about forty metres or just over twenty fathoms.

The first effect is a shortening and slowing of the waves, combined with a lessening of height so that a yacht making for the Elbe River from the west would find the sea becoming quieter after reaching the twenty fathom line some four or five miles short of the Elbe Lightship, depending upon the height of tide.

On nearing the shoals, the waves begin to increase their height, and as they continue to get shorter they will be getting steeper, changing their characters from approximately the shape of a sine curve to a series of isolated steep crests separated by long flat troughs. If at this stage the stream is ebbing fast from the Elbe River a particularly nasty sea will be

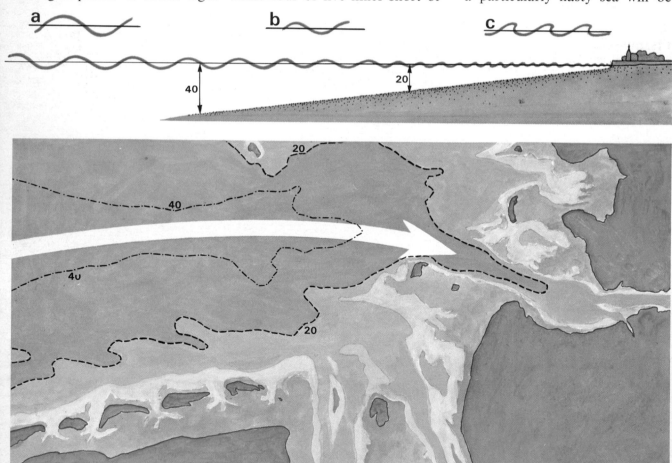

running without any increase in wind.

When a yacht is making for a harbour with a bar in the entrance, shallow water effect is particularly important, as the waves will rapidly steepen until the depth is down to about one and a half times the wave height, or even twice the wave height with an onshore gale, when they will break.

For example, a fresh wind blowing onshore for twelve hours might generate an average wave height of three metres in deep water, building up to some four metres before breaking when the depth was down to about six metres.

Sometimes, on a falling tide, the seas may begin to break as the tide level on the bar falls to the critical point of about one and a half times the wave height. At first only the biggest waves will be affected but as the tide continues to fall, more and more will break.

On coasts exposed to ocean waves the effect is apparent in much deeper water. Thus a moderate winter gale blowing in the Atlantic for twenty-four hours could build up seas with a mean wave height of six metres, which in shoaling water might increase to over eight metres. Waves would break on reaching double their depth, which in this case

1.16, 1.17 The wave character (**a**) changes as the boat approaches the coast, first becoming smaller and shorter (**b**), in this case at 40 metres depth. As shoals are reached, the waves steepen and then break (**c**), more so if the current is contrary.

1.18, 1.19 Waves breaking on the shallower parts of a coastal reef of the Hawaiian islands. The yacht is in a deeper channel. The critical depth (**d**) is one and a half times the wave height (**H**), or twice the wave height in onshore gales.

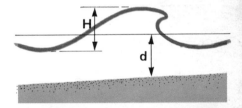

would be about the same as a ten fathom shoal.

Cliff effect

When there is relatively deep water right up to the foot of a cliff, then waves coming in at right angles to it will be reflected straight back. The same effect applies with waves pounding straight at a breakwater in fairly deep water.

The returning wave will inevitably have lost much of its energy against the cliff or breakwater, but if it comes head-on into collision with an incoming wave there will certainly be a furious battle between them. The sea will mount up almost vertically at the point of impact, and in an extreme case a small craft caught there could be rolled right over or overwhelmed.

The effect on a sea of reflected waves seldom extends far out from the cliff, so it can easily be avoided on passage by keeping more than half a mile to seawards.

The difficulty comes when a yacht wants to make for a harbour with waves reflecting back from cliffs either side, or a breakwater. All could be well until the final approach to the harbour entrance, when the seas suddenly become very dangerous.

1.20 Reflection off the base of a harbour mole causes a steep confused and very dangerous sea, but the rough water only extends a short distance off.

1.21 Just as safety is close at hand, the last hundred metres may be the most dangerous when it is too late to turn back.

Races

The most drastic effect is where uneven shoaling water and strong streams combine to make the seas especially turbulent. The cause is often a rocky submarine ridge extending seawards. This forces the stream to race round its end, jostling with the main stream, while the uneven shoaling causes overfalls, whirlpools, or huge standing waves.

Within such a race the water appears to boil to the surface, the disturbed area remaining in place relative to the land although the

1.22 Stream forced to concentrate, often on a submerged reef or promontory, will cause severely confused waves and overfalls.

water forming it pushes onwards. In very severe examples a small craft may be sucked into the bottom of a vortex and carried irresistibly onwards into a solid wall of water.

When primarily caused by the tidal stream, the whole race, with its gang of angry whirlpools may, at different stages of the tide, slowly move in relation to the land, and probably cease altogether with slack water, which may only last for a few minutes.

Tidal races are relatively innocuous at neap tides, but increase to their greatest vigour with the

spring tides. Should one of these coincide with a gale of wind, then the race is indeed a danger that could hazard vessels whatever their size. Small craft must take the greatest care to avoid getting into a situation where their own speed through the water is insufficient to prevent the tidal stream carrying them into the race.

1.23 This photograph, taken from a lifeboat, shows why the small craft should beware of crossing a bar in strong onshore winds and low tides.

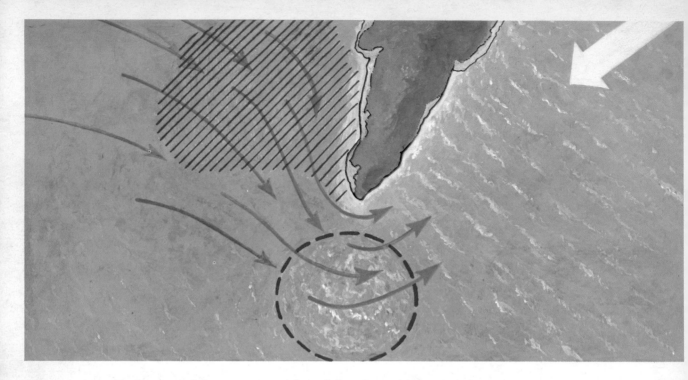

Races can also be caused by a semi-permanent current, perhaps when speeding up through a channel or when restricted by shallow waters. Thus in the Mediterranean channel between Tunisia and Sicily, westerly winds may bring the current near the Skerki Bank to a rate of nearly four knots, and, especially if the wind turns briskly to a new direction, a vigorous race forms in the relatively shallow water.

However, in the Mediterranean, even with so small a tidal range, the tidal streams may cause significant races. Famous in ancient mythology are the whirlpools of Scylla and Charybdis in the Straits of Messina. Although

24

an earthquake two centuries ago took away much of the effect of Scylla, the whirlpool which today forms off Torre Faro is the Charybdis of old. At spring tides, in a fresh wind, it can still be as dangerous to small craft in the Mediterranean as is The Race on the other side of the Atlantic through which twice each day millions of tons of water pour into Long Island Sound and back again.

Like the ancient Greeks, the Norse navigators, who crossed the Atlantic Ocean without fear, developed such awe for a tidal race in the Lofoten Islands that they created for the Maelstrom a myth of certain death to a mariner

1.24 A boat in the hatched area could be blanketed by high ground to windward and dragged by the current into the area of the race. Avoid such a trap by thinking ahead.

caught in it at any time. Today the yachtsman finds it dangerous at certain stages of a spring tide when it is accompanied by a strong north-west wind, but on other occasions a cruising yacht can navigate it with confidence.

Another cause of a race is conflict between currents running at different depths, especially if the sea bottom is uneven. Thus the rivers running into the Baltic tend to fill it to overflowing so that there is a constant current of almost fresh water setting

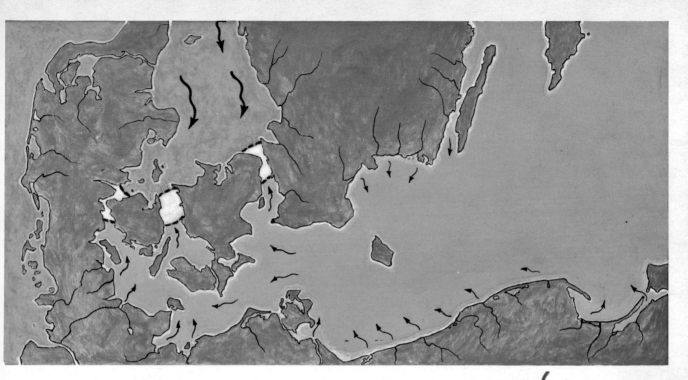

1.25 A steady outflow of fresh water from the Baltic meets, and rises above, the denser salt sea water in the shallow waters of the Belts, causing disturbed seas, indicated here by the pale band.

1.26 Tidal flow in and out of a restricted ▶ passage such as the entrance to Long Island Sound causes an important race to form at the narrowest part.

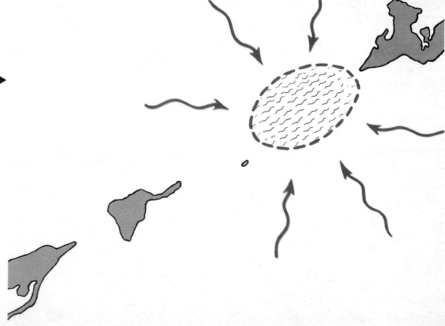

through the Great Belt towards the North Sea. At the same time seawater, which is heavier due to higher salt content, flows inwards as a deep water current beneath it. Conflict between these two currents may form a violent race on the surface when accompanied by a strong wind.

2 Rough weather dangers

2.1 Common reasons for this sort of emergency are:
  Unsecured safety harness
  A flogging headsail
  An unexpected gybe or roll
  Tripping over obstructions
  Slipping on wet decks, or on a sail or rope on the deck.

Falling overboard

In rough weather this is the greatest danger of all to those at sea in small craft. Among big seas anyone separated from a yacht is in real hazard and, even if firmly secured to the boat by safety harness, could well be injured before getting back on deck.

The danger is acute when the loss overboard of a member of the crew leaves her seriously shorthanded for the difficult job of picking him up. Even worse, the most experienced of helmsmen is useless for the recovery evolution if he is the one who is overboard, and has failed to give anyone else any practice beforehand.

A vital aspect of rough weather seamanship is that everyone outside the cabin should be properly secured to the yacht. This is largely a matter of habit, organization and planning. For example, the best safety equipment is useless if still in a locker down below when a surprise wave breaks over the foredeck just as someone is knocked off balance by a shaking headsail. Even sitting unsecured in the cockpit may be unsafe for someone not fully alert, especially if slightly seasick.

Personal safety equipment is dealt with in Chapter 6 and recovering a man overboard comes in Chapter 10.

Collision

Rough weather increases the danger of collision with other vessels from whom a small craft may be hidden in the trough of the waves often enough to make her unnoticed, especially at night and if her navigation lights are mounted low down.

She may not show up on the radar screen of a big ship among the wave echoes unless she carries an effective radar reflector at least fifteen feet above the deck.

The lookout from a yacht is usually bad, sails partly obscuring the view to leeward, while the wind and spray make it difficult to

2.2 Common reasons for this imminent danger are:
    Reduced crew efficiency due to cold, fatigue or seasickness
    Poor visibility due to flying spray and big seas
    Poor watch on the ship due to crew shortage, crew fatigue or over reliance on limited radar effectiveness

see to windward. Thus neither craft may be aware of the presence of the other until very close. By then immediate action may not be effective owing to the seas hindering her tacking, the wind force making a gybe dangerous, or the time taken for those below to don safety harness and get back up on deck being too long.

Running aground

This is a significant rough weather hazard as, in these conditions, visibility is often restricted by rain and spray. At the same time navigational accuracy may be seriously reduced by:

— Uncertain leeway
— Extra difficulty in steering
— The formidable task of taking good bearings when a boat is tossing violently
— The problem of plotting when the chart is wet
— Seasickness

An important part of the skill in rough weather is assessing the maximum error of the estimated position. The navigator is safe should he have assessed his maximum error as five miles when his actual error is four; yet with the same actual error he is in danger if he assumes that he knows where he is to within three.

A classic cause of marine

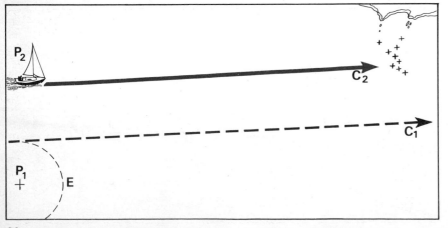

2.3, 2.4 Running aground in rough weather can be a real disaster, involving loss of the boat or even loss of life. In 2.4 the navigator estimated his position to be P_1 with an assumed circle of error, **E**. So he laid off course C_1 to clear the rocks. His actual position was P_2 owing to poor navigating conditions and so his track, C_2, put the yacht on the rocks.

casualties, even with large, well equipped ships manned by professional crews, is setting a course which converges on a lee shore with outlying hazards. The danger of such a course is much greater for a small yacht with modest equipment, limited lookout efficiency and far less experience of navigation.

Every landfall in rough weather needs particular care, and it may often be safest to heave-to well out to sea until conditions improve, or until those on board feel better able to deal with the problem.

Take as example a yacht which established her position precisely as she rounded a lightship *(2.5)*. She then set a course to pass outside a shoal buoy, allowing for the predicted tidal stream and the leeway previously experienced in that yacht.

In practice the strong wind had delayed the turn of the stream, so it was still setting round the line of the shoal against the yacht. Then with the wind and sea on the bow, under shortened sail, she was making much more leeway than expected.

It is difficult to see a small object looking into the wind and spray, while in this case the lookout was concentrated ahead and to leeward, where the buoy was expected. Thus the yacht might well have been on the shoal before sighting the buoy. Indeed there have been frequent cases where, after grounding, the buoy previously unnoticed was seen not far off.

Frequent back bearings on the lightship astern, so long as it remained visible, might have given a clue as to what was happening. If the time had been noted on passing the lightship, and the buoy was not sighted at the time plotted, it would have shown that something was wrong, with at least a hint that the stream was not setting as predicted.

Yet most important of all, soundings taken regularly would almost certainly have given warning before coming onto such a shoal.

However, all these seamanlike precautions are difficult and irksome in rough weather, so the good seaman should appreciate his limitations and only attempt such a course if confident in all departments:
— Accurate steering
— Good lookouts
— Reliable sounding equipment
— Ability to tack instantly

2.5 The actual current, C_2, was not as predicted, C_1, due to strong prevailing wind. In addition leeway was greater than usual owing to slow progress against wind and sea. Therefore the course laid put the yacht on the shoal at **X**. Back bearings on the lightship would have shown up the mistake.

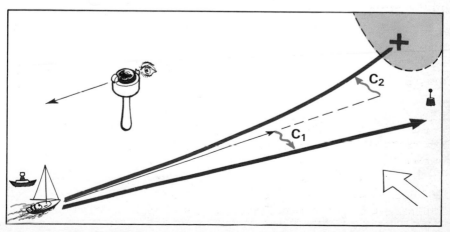

Pooping

A vessel is pooped when a wave breaks over her stern, or poop. It may mean no more than a half-filled cockpit, such as is readily accepted by a strong crew properly secured to the boat by safety gear, and with the boat well battened down to prevent water going below. But she could be swept by so violent a rush of water that control is lost, equipment is damaged and perhaps even a hatch is stove in.

Only in the early stages of a strong wind will a sailing yacht be able to keep ahead of the waves by means of her own speed. Starting from a calm tideless sea, two hours of a force 7 wind will cause the average speed of the waves to reach over ten knots, making them faster than most cruising yachts can run before the wind. If the waves were already moving in the same direction from a previous breeze, two hours of force 7 could well bring them to an average speed of some fifteen knots, so that even a light displacement planing craft would be unlikely to outsail them.

Pooping may be caused by the breaking top of a wave exceeding the height of the yacht's freeboard aft, or by the yacht's pitch carrying her stern down into an overtaking wave. In both cases high freeboard aft is a positive factor against pooping, but is not complete protection.

Until a gale has been blowing for many hours the breaking tops of waves in the open sea are unlikely to exceed the height of even a small cruising yacht's freeboard, unless they are affected by something other than the wind itself, such as shoaling, a contrary stream or current, a rapid change of wind direction, wash from a passing ship, or even wake from the yacht herself.

Wake increases with speed, so that the higher the yacht's speed the more likely is her wake to steepen the top of a following wave and assist it to break just in the position that floods over the stern. Streaming warps (see page 114) will push the wake further aft and help to break the waves well clear of the stern.

Pitching is controlled by the yacht's hull shape and the position of weights within her. Weights at the extremes, forward and aft, make her stern slower to rise to a following wave, so heavy equipment, spare gear and crew should be concentrated amidships.

The momentum of a pitch is proportional to the square of its velocity; yet this pitch velocity depends less on the speed of the yacht through the water than on the difference between its speed and that of the wave. With regular waves the yacht's speed may reduce, rather than increase, the liability to the type of pooping due to the stern pitching into a following sea. However, a rough sea is far from a regular pattern of waves, so in practice fast sailing before a following sea needs great skill, while the higher the boat's speed the more damaging is the result if she gets out of step.

Thus, speed when running before a sea, makes the first type of pooping more likely and is an unreliable help against the second type. The decision when to ease speed must depend largely on experience. The helmsman who knows his boat well in rough seas can gauge the feel of her movement and know when she is beginning to get 'above herself'.

Without such experience it is wise to exercise caution. A heavy pooping as the first warning that the following seas are too much for her can be thoroughly demoralizing, especially when no-one on board has experienced this before. Yet it may be no more than exciting to a skilled crew who know their own ability and the strength of their well tuned gear.

2.6 The main cause of pooping is a big wave breaking over the stern. The boat cannot escape by her speed, indeed her stern wave can trigger off the breaking crest.

2.7 A yacht pitches by oscillating about her centre of gravity. Extra weight in the ends of the hull means slowed reaction to an approaching wave especially if it is out of phase with the pitch.

Broaching-to

A yacht may broach-to when running fast before a strong wind and steep sea. A broach starts as the front of a wave lifts and carries forward the stern of the yacht, while her bows are buried in the trough. The momentum increases the angle of heel, while sail pressure completes the job by adding a further strong turning moment which the helm is totally unable to counter. She is completely out of control and may be forced right over onto her beam ends with the whole of her mast in the water.

Skilful steering, anticipating trouble, coupled with good sail trimming, will postpone the start of broaching in a rising sea. Indeed the superhelmsman backed by an experienced sail trimmer, both having a highly developed feel for the boat, can keep her going, just as a top steeple-chase jockey will clear many more fences that others, before he takes his toss.

A broach need not in itself be dangerous but it is something to avoid in a cruising boat lacking a strong and experienced crew to sort out the problems that may follow. It will seize on any flaws in the boat; the violent slew onto her side, skidding through the water with the mast and sails in the sea, with half the deck underwater, will search out any weakness and can sometimes result in the loss of a mast.

Below decks it will be far from pleasant for someone hurled out of a weather bunk or for another who sees a carefully prepared and nearly cooked meal plastered over the cabin side.

The preventative for broaching is less sail and less speed, perhaps even heaving-to or streaming warps (see chapter 9).

2.8 A yacht broaches in a following sea when the forces on rig and hull become out of balance. The stern is lifted by a wave, she heels excessively, the bow digs in and the sail force acts to one side, all combining to throw her irresistibly round and onto her beam-ends.

Overwhelming

In certain conditions, seas can become so high and steep as to endanger a yacht by overwhelming it with the sheer weight and momentum of water crashing down on the coachroof and deck.

Outside the areas of hurricanes and other tropical revolving storms, or severe winter gales, such seas are in effect confined to a combination of gale and race (see page 23), or shallow water; thus they will often be close to the land.

In a gale, the headland which a yacht might be striving to round for shelter, or the harbour entrance through which she seeks safety, may be the most dangerous waters of all. Even lifeboats designed to rescue those on the seas during storm conditions, manned by those with expert local knowledge, have sometimes met with disaster when nearly back in harbour. The coxswain had to decide whether to risk being overwhelmed off the entrance, or whether to stay at sea with survivors on board needing medical attention.

Unless the skipper of a yacht is faced with a similarly agonizing quandary he should, in a gale, firmly decide to stay well away from the lee shore. It will be no easy decision when all on board are clamouring for harbour. Viewed from up-wind the seas may look moderate; the full violence cannot usually be judged until the yacht is already in danger and unable to turn back seaward.

2.9 A painting based on a photograph taken from a Soviet ship of a freak wave overwhelming the Frazerburgh lifeboat. The fishing boat *Opal* is in the foreground.

Speed

Sailing fast certainly adds to the dangers of rough weather.

Beating to windward the yacht will pound into the seas the more violently the faster she is going; even leaping off the crests to crash into the face of the next wave ahead. This adds to discomfort down below, and makes it wetter on deck; it also puts an increasing strain on the hull. A further hazard is the greater possibility of somebody being thrown overboard.

Broad reaching with the wind just abaft the beam, the yacht will be more comfortable in the same conditions, until sometimes a combination of high speed and the wave formation together with pressure on the sails, sets up a violent rolling motion which may dip the main boom into the sea. Again, the gear will suffer; and again, the crew are in danger.

Speed, when running before the wind, is a contributory cause of broaching, and the faster the speed the more damage a broach will cause. As has been previously shown, in some circumstances high speed makes pooping more likely, the wake causing a following sea to mount up and break, perhaps cascading right over her stern.

Yet speed also has its safety

factor in making it possible to avoid a dangerous situation. For example pressing on under a full spread of canvas could enable a yacht to sail clear when she might have been carried by the tidal stream into a heavy race, if reefed right down.

Thus danger in rough weather comes from a wrong use of speed: not using speed when speed is required, or failing to slow down when speed becomes dangerous.

Beware of leaving full sail set in freshening weather until it is difficult, or even dangerous, to reduce it with the particular crew strength available. Even those of powerful physique, good balance and long experience of sheltered water sailing, can be no more than a thoroughly weak crew when tired, seasick and unfamiliar with the rough conditions. Watch the weather signs and do not miss the forecasts. Then change down or reef early.

Another point to watch is the quality of helmsmanship. A skipper may believe that all is well when a boat is travelling fast and riding the seas easily in the expert hands of a good rough sea helmsman. This may change dramatically when the next watch takes over and a less experienced man is on the helm.

2.10 Speed, causing excessive rolling, can lead in turn to broken gear.

2.11 When huge seas start to break, it is ▶ time to reduce speed.

Effects on a boat

The sheer weight of water in a wave moving fast under wind pressure can smash the strongest structure. One only has to look at the damage that constantly occurs to stone breakwaters, solid sea walls and steel piers. A yacht is comparatively light, buoyant and yielding and so normally does not come to much harm. However, an awkward or breaking wave, or a strong gust of wind blasting at a boat with too much sail set, can still do a great deal of damage of which that in the photo is typical.

Sail failure

Properly handled and well maintained sails are amazingly strong, but any sail may fail if used in conditions which will load it above its designed strength.

It might not be realized that a sail encounters much heavier strains when being lowered, especially by a crew of modest strength,

3.1 The power of a wave, increased by the speed of the boat, can cause tremendous loads on the whole structure.

than it does while full of wind while correctly set. The inevitable flogging can do a great deal of damage to the sail material and can even destroy the cloth or break the seaming by battering it against the mast or other fixed obstruction.

The sail must be lowered fast, and if there is only one person on deck to lower and gather the sail, with the helmsman only able to give slight help from the cockpit, then it must be done much sooner than if there is a strong team to smother it as it comes down.

When lowering a headsail in strong winds, the sheet should be turned up, so that at least the foot of the sail remains under control. As soon as the halyard starts to be eased, the leech will begin to flog with great violence and, apart from damage to the sail itself, it can hurt, or even whip someone overboard. The safest place on the foredeck, even though it is also the wettest, is within the pulpit with safety harness hooked on. Standing is often too insecure, but it is often possible to sit on deck with both feet getting a good grip and the hands free to haul down and secure the sail as it is lowered. Sail ties should always be to hand to muzzle the sail.

3.3 Sail ties should always be to hand. ▶

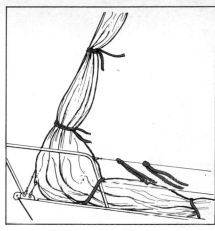

3.2 The safest, if the wettest, place to muzzle the headsail is wedged into the pulpit with safety harness clipped on.

If a sail should fail when actually set it is usually a seam that goes, and this will run unless it can be lowered properly. Easing the sheet can temporarily reduce the strain so long as the sail is not allowed to flap. When ready to lower, gather the sail in quickly so that its flapping does not increase the split.

A common place for a mainsail to split is near the foot, caused by abrasion and projections on the boom when reefed. The immediate answer may be to reef sufficiently to cover up the split. Another common place for a split to start is on the leech itself, but this means a major repair because the loading here is particularly high.

A tear in the material itself is unlikely unless the sail has fouled something sharp, and a small tear may go unnoticed for some time without getting any worse; yet it is a weakness which might turn into a split, so the wise seaman keeps a close eye for even the smallest tear and darns it or replaces the sail at the first opportunity.

A well made sail is strengthened at all stress points, so the headboard and the cringles at the tack and clew are only likely to go if the sail is badly worn. Prevention of trouble is a matter of regular inspection.

In spite of this, should a headboard let go, the sail will come down with a run and this, in itself,

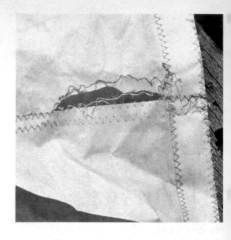

should not cause too much trouble. The problem will be that the halyard, and whatever remains attached to it, will still be at the masthead with no means of hauling it down.

A personal visit aloft in rough conditions is unlikely to be welcome, especially if the only halyard available means that no sail can remain set to steady the boat. An alternative is to use the burgee halyard or the main boom topping lift to hoist aloft a small grapnel, or a boat hook, and to 'fish' with this for the mast-headed gear. It is essential to rig a downhaul line as otherwise yet more gear will be stuck aloft.

Should a headsail clew tear away, the rest of the sail will set up violent flogging which will shake the whole boat and certainly cause enormous strains both on the sail itself and the whole rigging. If close-hauled at the time, even moving forward on deck to the halyard may invite a severe clout on the head from the loose sail. The answer is to steer the boat off the wind to keep the sail well out over the side. It should then be lowered as quickly as possible. If reef cringles are fitted it may be possible to rehoist the same sail with a reef tucked in.

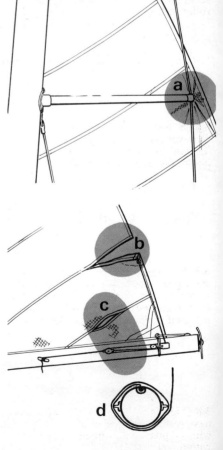

3.4 Modern sailcloth is so hard that the stitching remains proud of the surface and is vulnerable to chafe. Constant watch must be kept for worn threads which must be replaced immediately.

3.5 Common failure points are on the headsail leach, where it rubs the spreaders (**a**), on the mainsail leach, where the load is particularly heavy (**b**), on mainsail seams, where boom fittings catch when roller reefing (**c & d**).

3.6 A lost halyard can sometimes be ▶ retrieved without going up the mast, by 'fishing' for it with a grapnel or a boat hook hoisted on another halyard.

3.7 (Far right, top) If a headsail clew or sheet goes, the boat should immediately be put off the wind so that the sail is in the lee and can be retrieved without damaging itself further or injuring the crew.

3.8 (Far right, bottom) Many headsails have reefing cringles, in which case a sail with a damaged tack or clew can be re-set with a reef tucked in.

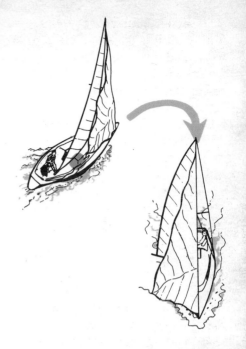

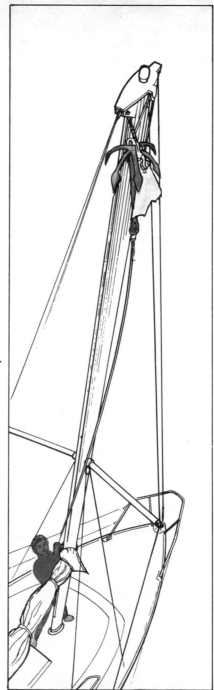

Damage to ropes and gear

Rough weather puts extra strains on gear, particularly when not correctly used. For example if, in a following sea, the main boom is allowed to swing unchecked, the gooseneck fitting at the mast end, or the sheet fitting at the clew may suffer such heavy strains from snubbing that it may fail.

Similarly, the headsail may be alternating between flapping as it is blanketed by the mainsail and filling again with a crack like a gun shot; this puts severe strain on the sail, its hanks, and also on the block which leads its sheet to the winch. Sometimes the headsail will fill with such violence that the whole boat is shaken and every part of the standing rigging is shocked.

Shackles can be relied upon to stand up to their tested strength if properly used. However if the pin has not been screwed or twisted to the full extent, the jerks of bad weather sailing may well work it out, so that the shackle lets go. A shackle, hank or sail slide, previously knocked partly out of shape or worn, will also have lost much of its strength and may break. Even one shackle failing can be the start of a train of bad weather incidents leading to a serious situation.

A sheet led foul of any sharp obstruction will quickly wear through under the constant and

3.9 A fore guy led from the boom end and firmly secured forward will prevent the boom swinging and snatching when the boat rolls. Better, lead the guy through a block forward and cleat it within reach of the cockpit so that it can be let go in an emergency.

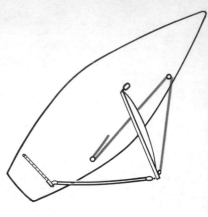

3.10 A partly blanketed headsail can be a danger, alternately backing and filling with violence. Either luff slightly to fill it or reef the mainsail to give it clearer air.

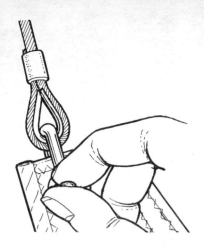

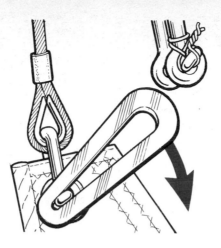

3.11 Galvanized shackles become slightly stiff due to rusting, but stainless shackles are always free and can shake loose easily. Always tighten with a spanner, or mouse them with wire.

3.13 A broken mainsheet block is no emergency, but can lead to danger if the boom is not secured. Steer across the wind. Ease the halyard and topping lift, or drop the sail entirely and furl it. Secure the boom to the guard rails and then work on it in safety from the cockpit.

3.12 Constantly check all fittings. An overstrained or worn sail slide, like this one, could lead to a chain of breakages if it lets go in a hard wind.

varying strains of hard weather. A broken sheet leaves the boat with reduced motive power though, in the case of a headsail, the boat can be tacked to bring the other side into use until a repair can be made.

The main sheet itself seldom breaks as the strain on each part of the rope is much less than on a single part fore sheet which is usually tensioned by a winch. However, should the block or its tang break, its boom will be free to swing around and be a menace to anyone on deck or who is trying to control it.

Damage to the rig

If properly designed and fitted, the standing rigging will be strong enough for the whole boat to be lifted out by its masthead. Yet if any one of the individual stays, shrouds, spreaders, or fittings should fail there is danger of the mast collapsing under the strains of heavy weather.

Common failures are:
— A broken spreader
— A pulled splice
— A cracked tang
— A lost split-pin
— A broken wire
— A bent or damaged turnbuckle, shackle or chainplate.

All these failures can be prevented by regular attention, not only when fitting out, but also each time before going to sea.

Damage leading to rigging failure often actually starts with a minor incident in harbour, although the failure itself may only happen under the severe testing of bad weather.

Spreaders are particularly vulnerable in harbour. Two sailing yachts lying together with their masts in line may clash spreaders due to the wash of a passing craft—perhaps even a small motorboat.

Unnoticed damage can also happen when manoeuvring alongside a high wharf, or perhaps a wharf with an overhanging crane. While intent on things at eye level, such as coming alongside smoothly and securing the berthing warps, it might not be seen that the spreader or some part of the rigging has fouled an overhead obstruction. An unfair sideways strain might fracture the bolts holding the spreader to the mast fitting for example.

Other causes of damage to rigging could well happen when no-one is on board. Another craft may come alongside too fast and one of her crew take a turn around your rigging screw with a berthing line; this may stop his boat, but at the expense of crippling your turnbuckle or rigging screw. The trouble is that no-one on board the offending yacht may realize what damage they have done.

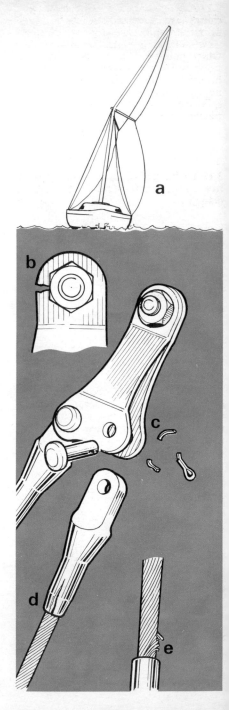

3.14 A broken or dislodged spreader will cause the mast to bend or collapse, as well as overstraining other rigging or fittings which may fail under stress later (**a**). Other points to watch for on routine inspections are: cracks in tangs (**b**), broken or loose retaining pins or lock-nuts (**c**), corroded or cracked clamp splices (**d**), broken strands of wire (**e**), bent rigging screws (**f**).

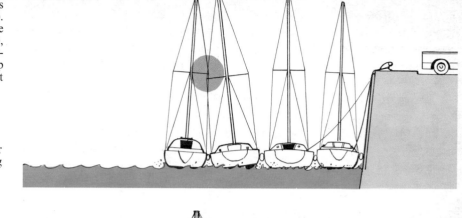

3.15 Yachts tied up together at a wall or trot are most vulnerable to rigging damage.

3.16 Moor with masts out of line to minimize the danger.

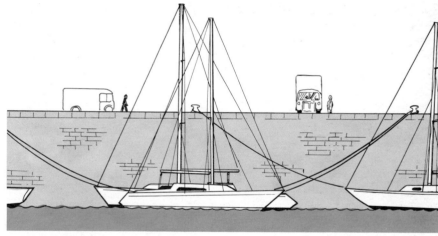

3.17 Make sure that adjacent yachts cannot move fore-and-aft relative to each other by attention to bow and stern lines (**a**) and by fitting good springs (**b**). Keep masts well apart laterally (**d**).

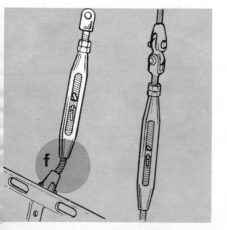

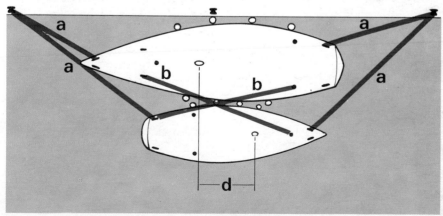

Dismasting

Should a cap shroud let go the mast will probably bend above the lower shrouds until it buckles, if a metal mast, or splinters if made of wood. The actual bending is quite a slow process, which takes away the sense of catastrophe, yet once it starts even the most alert helmsman is unlikely to be able to stop it by tacking or gybing to bring the wind on the other side.

A mast stepped below will probably collapse a few feet above the deck, perhaps leaving the boom intact, but more often taking the gooseneck and boom with it. If stepped on deck, the whole rig may go over the side complete, remaining secured to the boat by a jumble of wires and ropes.

Dismasting in rough weather is alarming but, unless associated with some other misfortune such as broaching or overwhelming, it should not be disastrous. In fact the first reaction after dismasting is usually one of relieved surprise that the whole process was not more violent. Dismasting disables a sailing craft's main means of progress, yet with enough sea room to leeward this aspect can

wait until conditions improve; but other matters may call for immediate attention.

Before rushing into action after a dismasting, the skipper must assess the priorities. The chief dangers are:

— Spars damaging the hull
— The jumble of wreckage injuring those struggling to put things right
— Loose rigging getting round the propeller
— Drifting into shoal or dangerous water

A mast, boom or spreader, especially with a jagged end, might make a hole right through the hull if the boat is thrown by a wave hard against it; loose spars could certainly damage the boat in other ways or crush the limbs of the crew. Rigging looks so neat and simple when in its proper place, but turns into an apparently impossible muddle when mast, sails and all are tossing about alongside in a rough sea. Where any wire rigging is left leading across the deck it is liable to jerk taut as the boat rolls, cutting right through a finger that is caught holding it.

3.18 A dismasted yacht is a mess and, at least temporarily, is immobile. Though the matter needs immediate attention to avoid further damage, it is not normally an emergency.

Without the weight of the rig, the boat will rise higher out of the water than usual and her roll will be quicker. It will need a thoroughly strong crew, besides a great deal of time, to haul mast, boom and sail safely on board. In most cruising boats this is quite impracticable, at least until the sea begins to moderate.

If there is danger of holing the hull, correcting this must have first priority. Usually, all that can be done immediately is to secure with ropes the wayward spar, to give time for a complete assessment. Occasionally the matter is so serious that it will have to be cut adrift without delay.

When the danger of damage to the hull is no longer pressing it is time to think and plan rather than rush into premature action. There will be a long job ahead. Most crews would then greatly benefit from a hot drink all round, accompanied by a quiet discussion. Ten minutes given over to this might save hours in the end, and enable a more detached view to be taken of the disaster.

Next assemble the available tools. If space has been found on board for heavy wire cutters and a

3.19 Two ways of dealing with rigging. **a)** Cut the wires with heavy wire cutters which should be part of the tool kit. **b)** Ease the strain with a stopper taken to a winch and then release the end fitting.

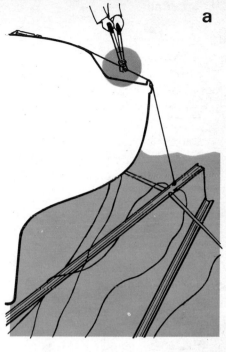

hacksaw, they will truly demonstrate their worth. In weather bad enough to eliminate the chance of hauling everything on board, the aim must be to unshackle or cut all the rigging except that by which the boat can lie to the rig as a sea anchor, whether it remains afloat or not.

The plan must decide whether it is intended to lie by the bow or the stern; this will depend largely on what rigging is left and what can be got at in the circumstances. The forestay is one of the stronger rigging wires and will already be secured right in the eyes of the boat, so this could be a good starting point. Without the windage of the mast, the yacht should lie reasonably well head on to the wind and seas, with the wreck of the rig out ahead. Riding stern first, the boat may be steadier, but it exposes her rudder to the force of an oncoming wave which can be more damaging when the drag of the wreckage allows little give.

Whether lying to the wreckage ahead or astern it is vital to be able to slip it in an emergency. It is also

vital not to turn the engine over until it is certain that the boat is clear of all rigging. A rope round the propeller in rough weather will almost certainly disable the dismasted yacht completely.

If there is immediate danger to leeward, then of course an attempt must be made to motor. However, if help is coming and there seems a good chance of salvaging the mast and rig, then it may be best to secure it all alongside, taking care there is no projection which could hole the hull.

3.20 The rig can act as a sea anchor until the sea moderates or help comes.

3.21 Do not turn the propeller until all ropes and wires are clear.

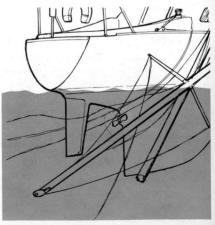

Security below decks

The pitching and slamming of a boat going to windward in bad seas will seek out any gear which is defective or inadequately secured and may cause quite as much trouble as gear failure on deck *(3.22)*.

The galley is one area of potential danger. Not only can the violent motion dislodge parts of the stove not properly fixed, but the whole stove itself may come adrift. Just as serious is a hot cooking pot which can fly off and spray its contents over everything.

Such relatively minor failures below can become serious by setting off a train of accidents leading, for example, to a bad burn for the person trying to catch a hot saucepan. One person could be disabled, and another be fully occupied dressing the burn, at a time when help is suddenly needed on deck. The failure to answer the urgent call might distract the attention of the helmsman, who gybes all standing and splits the mainsail. Rough weather needs a cool head!

Well found yachts will have basic security devices built in, such as non-opening drawers and safety cupboard catches, but a pile of tins being hurled about can break any door and the thump of the hull crashing into the trough can lift heavy objects off their seatings.

So, before rough weather arrives:
— Secure anything movable
— Put books, food and small objects in lockers or on the cabin floor
— Check security of batteries, water containers, bottles, stove, floor boards, anchor and chain and lash them down if in any doubt

3.22 It is too late to secure below after the onset of rough weather. In a very short time the cabin can become a shambles causing many problems and thoroughly demoralizing the crew.

Steering breakdown

Jammed steering in rough weather is an emergency. It usually follows on a broach or some violent movement of the yacht and can be a result of extra strain on the steering gear itself, or a lurch causing something to jam.

The most effective immediate action is to heave-to (see also page 112), if practicable with the backed headsail on the same side to which the rudder is jammed. This will steady the boat and give tolerable conditions for repairs as well as preventing her from getting into any further trouble.

With wheel steering the cause will often be something preventing movement of the quadrant or a rope jamming the steering wire block. Such a jam could entail a lengthy job cutting the rope clear in a cramped position within the after locker. This will test personal immunity to seasickness severely.

Tiller steering is less likely to jam, but the tiller can easily be broken, perhaps by someone falling heavily against it with a lurch of the boat. In such a case the rudder will still be free and if a spare tiller is carried it will just be a matter of changing to that, but failing this a jury tiller can often be rigged.

3.23 Possible methods of fixing a jury tiller to an outboard rudder (left) and an inboard metal stock (right).

If the rudder post is accessible and is made with a hole into which the tiller slots, then a piece of wood, such as a broom handle, can be shaved down until it fits. If this is not possible, two pieces of wood or metal with flat surfaces might be lashed tightly together to get a firm grip on the rectangular head.

In counter-steered boats, a broken tiller fitting may leave only the square metal head of the rubber stock protruding a few inches from the bottom of the cockpit. A large adjustable spanner may be able to grip this, with the broken tiller, or perhaps a broom handle, lashed to it to give leverage.

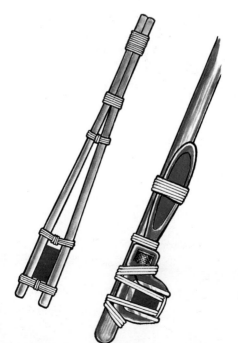

Other cases can be solved only by the mechanical ingenuity which is as much a part of rough weather seamanship as is skill in steering or handling sails. Yet such ingenuity flourishes best in moderate conditions, so it is wise to work out, when safe in harbour, how to deal with a failure in your particular boat should it occur in rough weather.

Steering without a rudder is usually quite practicable in a well balanced yacht under sail. However it is likely to need close attention on deck and possibly some co-operation down below.

Apart from balancing the rig, fore and aft positioning of weight will have an effect on the trim. More weight forward will lift the stern and cause the boat to tend to luff, and vice versa. The easiest weight to move is usually human weight. Someone sleeping in the quarter berth moving to the fore cabin will have an appreciable effect and will tend to increase weather helm.

One can usually only sail on a narrow range of courses from fairly close hauled to a beam reach when using fore-and-aft sails, even with constant attention to the sheets as well; for downwind courses twin headsails or the spinnaker could provide the answer.

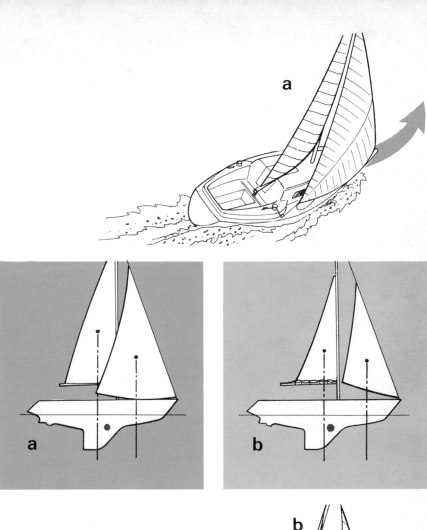

a

a

b

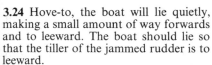

3.24 Hove-to, the boat will lie quietly, making a small amount of way forwards and to leeward. The boat should lie so that the tiller of the jammed rudder is to leeward.

3.25 With the rudder swinging free, or with no rudder at all, one has to balance the rig so that it acts coincidentally with the centre of lateral resistance of the hull. Normally sheeted, the sail plan is acting too far aft and the boat luffs (**a**). Best results will be obtained with a smaller headsail and a well reefed mainsail to slow the boat. Ease the mainsheet, and possibly the jib sheet too, until the course remains steady (**b**).

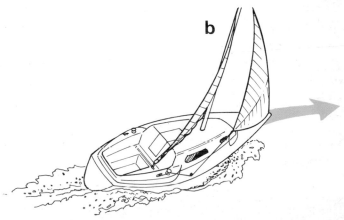

b

Jury rudder

There are several ways of steering should the boat be reluctant to hold the course required solely by adjusting sail trim.

A jury steering oar is one possibility. Even if only a short dinghy paddle is available this can be lengthened by lashing a spinnaker pole to it, or a piece of floorboard.

This built-up spar is then lashed right aft to serve as a rudder to steer the boat. If the lashing is arranged so that the spar can twist, the blade can feather when there is no need to apply helm.

Another method is to drag astern a length of rope, or even a canvas bucket, rigged so that the point of tow can be adjusted from outside one quarter to outside the other.

A further elaboration is to lash a spinnaker pole across the stern so that two towed lines can be led through the ends without the need to rig blocks.

Remember to put a figure-of-eight knot in each line, so that if a rope is mistakenly let go it does not disappear astern.

The lines can be led to a sheet winch, or if none is free, to a cleat. Then by hauling in one or the other the boat can be steered. A downwind course is easy with such systems and may even be possible with the mainsail set.

3.26 Alternative methods of steering. Top: the drag-line is winched to one quarter or the other. A length of rope may be sufficient but, if necessary, extra resistance, and hence turning effort, may be obtained from a canvas bucket or coil of rope.

Lower drawing: the built-up spar can be very effective as an emergency rudder.

Flooding

Apart from damage causing a hole in the hull, water can flood into a boat from:

— Leaks above the waterline, which need noting for later attention in harbour.
— Leaks below the waterline, which need immediate attention.
— Designed openings, such as hatches and portlights which have been left open.

In rough seas leaks which were hardly noticeable before will increase greatly due to the extra strains on the hull, and also due to the sheer force of the waves and spray.

Leaks often appear to be much worse than they really are since only a few pints of water hurled violently about the cabin can give the impression of many gallons.

The more water there is in the boat the harder it is to trace the cause of the leaks. Thus it is important to pump the bilges dry before going to sea, and to keep them as dry as possible by regular inspection and pumping. Any leak is then more easily found.

Leaks above the waterline may enter round the mast, if this passes through the deck, or via cracks in the decks, the joint between deck and hull, or from ill-fitting hatches or perished portlight rubbers.

Rough weather is a poor time for stopping any minor leak, but it is a good time to record them, as memories will rapidly dissolve before reaching harbour. Meantime the best that can be done is to improvise some means of diverting the drips from a bunk or chart table, perhaps using a strip of sail material kept for repairs, or a polythene sheet.

Leaks below water level are difficult to trace in rough conditions, partly owing to water sloshing around, and partly because their positions in the bilges or behind the engine may be inaccessible.

All hull fittings such as engine cooling water inlets, sink and cockpit drains, heads' inlets and outlets, must be suspect. Most will have sea-cocks just inside the hull and so can be shut off if a leak in the system is found. However once shut off the system is then out of action.

A common place for increased leaking in rough weather is the

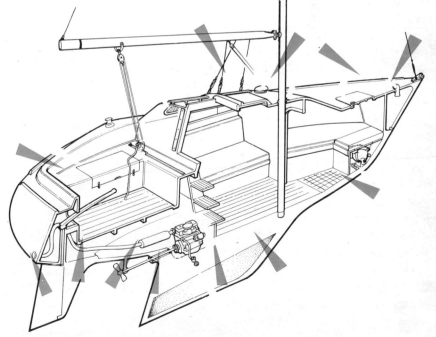

3.27 Common sources of leaks are: Above water level—windows, ventilators, mast coat, hatches, navel pipe, chain plates, engine exhaust. Below water—rudder trunk, propeller shaft, sea-cocks.

stern tube. It is seldom easy to tighten the shaft gland nut in those conditions but screwing down on the stern tube greaser may reduce the leak.

It should never happen, but there have been too many cases of the propeller shaft coming uncoupled from the drive so that propeller and tail shaft work their way out to leave the stern tube open for the sea to rush in. The loose shaft has also been known to jam the rudder.

This is a drastic situation and immediate action might be a rag draped over the end of a boathook or broom handle and pushed into the opening to check the flow. Meantime a wooden plug could be cut from the loom of an oar, then well greased and driven into the hole. Some boats carry a set of conical shaped softwood plugs for blocking holes such as this.

The most common way of all for water to get below is through the designed openings. Least obvious of these is the navel pipe through which the anchor cable is led on deck. When water comes 'green' over the foredeck a good deal of sea will get below unless the navel pipe has previously been plugged.

At sea portlights should be screwed tight shut. Should it be necessary to open one, great care should be taken to shut it again before water, or even spray, comes on deck. The most likely port to be overlooked is in the heads, and there is a soaking for anyone who uses this.

Each time someone goes below in rough weather a good deal of water reaches the cabin on the oilskins, but it becomes a torrent if someone is caught half-way down the hatch when a wave hurtles over the coachroof and reflects off him into the cabin. A hood over the hatch will reduce this problem.

Most drastic of all flooding comes from pooping with a hatch fully open. Hatches in a cruising boat are normally designed to open towards the stern, so a big wave rolling in from aft will pour down into the cabin in a real torrent, especially if it is the main companionway hatch that is open.

It is bad to find the cabin half full of water in a gale, but seldom quite as bad as it seems, as a boat can take a great deal of water before she is in real danger of foundering. However, with enough water aboard her stability will be greatly reduced; so, after shutting the hatch to prevent the next wave going below, the immediate action is to reduce sail quickly. That done, the boat in her waterlogged state will quickly lose speed, and this alone will greatly reduce the chance of being pooped again.

3.28 A pooping can be a frightening experience and is a warning that the yacht has too much speed. It can be disastrous if the cockpit crew are not well secured by lifelines, and will also flood the cabin if the main hatch is open.

3.29 A spray hood (left) allows ventilation and entry, at the same time protecting the interior of the cabin from a soaking by spray. In any case the main hatch should be shuttered when running before a heavy breaking sea (right).

Getting water out

A frightened man with a bucket is usually the quickest method of getting water out of a sailing boat. When the water is deep enough below no hand-worked pump will do better, and a bucket cannot get blocked!

When more than one person is on the job, canvas or plastic buckets are particularly suitable as they hurt less than rigid ones when a lurch of the boat hurls the bucket into the face. So long as the cockpit is self-draining, which it ought to be for any boat sailing offshore, time can be saved by emptying buckets straight into it to drain away.

Once the water level is down to near the cabin sole, a good bilge pump is best to finish off the job. However a boat full of water being tossed about in a rough sea will almost certainly collect a variety of things dislodged from where they should have been stowed. Once pumping starts, at least some of the debris will be attracted to the pump suction and either block it completely or at least make pumping harder work. This will mean grovelling in the bilges to clear the suction pipe or the strum box time and again. Apart from the delay, this is such an unpleasant job that it will certainly prompt a devout resolution to stow things more carefully in future.

3.30 A frightened man with a bucket is the fastest way of getting out water.

3.31 The bilge pump outlet should have an anti-syphon loop above the waterline. If the strainer on the inlet can be lifted up it will be far easier to clear it of debris when blocked.

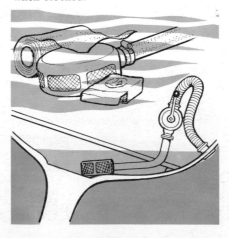

Holed

The hull can be holed by collision with another craft, by hitting floating wreckage, by a rock or even by running into a whale. Rough weather is only one of the factors which might lead to holing, but inevitably it will mean that the action demanded will be more difficult. Many yachts have got back to safety even with large holes in the hull. 'Galway Blazer II' was sailing far from the land when a Great White Shark smashed into her side underwater. Her single-handed skipper immediately put her about on the other tack, whereupon the strong wind heeled her over to keep the hole mainly out of the water. Nevertheless a ton or so of the sea got into the boat before effective repairs were made, but she was afloat!

Some yachts carry cans of chemical which, when mixed, swell to form an expanded plastic foam to give extra buoyancy. In a particular twenty four foot glass fibre sailing cruiser, the space under her two main berths, each just over six feet long could, when filled with plastic foam, keep her afloat complete with the keel, engine, stores, equipment and her four crew. But the crew would be scarcely out of the water and the boat would have to carry six gallons of the unmixed chemical which would take several minutes to set and meantime might be washed away by the incoming sea.

The first effort should be to check the water coming in. A blanket or cushion pushed into the hole will greatly reduce the inflow of water, especially if it can be brought above the waterline by heeling the boat. The problem is usually to get at the hole from inside, especially if it should be in a seat locker full of stores.

Any temporary cover from outside the hole will have the advantage that the pressure of the sea will tend to press it against the hull. The main difficulty is actually to place some object, such as a sail, over the hole and to keep it in position, especially when the shape of the hull prevents a rope passed under the keel from holding the sail tight against the hull.

A headsail could be best for this method, especially because its

wire luff can be hove taut on a winch. Alternately the luff can be secured with hanks to the rail and the sheet passed under the hull and pulled taut.

The rolling of the boat, the breaking seas and the quantity of water below make the situation doubly frightening. So, as always, one should try to keep a cool head and think before acting.

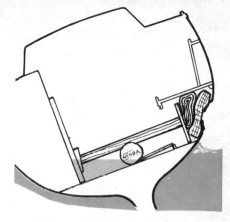

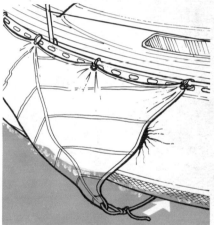

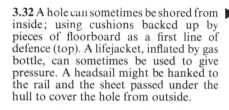

3.32 A hole can sometimes be shored from inside; using cushions backed up by pieces of floorboard as a first line of defence (top). A lifejacket, inflated by gas bottle, can sometimes be used to give pressure. A headsail might be hanked to the rail and the sheet passed under the hull to cover the hole from outside.

3.33 and **3.34** *Galway Blazer II*, sailed single-handed, reached port with this temporary patch fifteen days after a collision with a shark in deep ocean.

4 Effects on the crew

Bad weather inevitably brings a higher risk of problems for the people on board. Obviously they are likely to be wetter and colder so that extra precautions are needed to keep dry and warm *before* the first splash lands in the cockpit.

Other hazards include not only the ever present risk of injury to limbs and body but those associated with fatigue, mental confusion and, of course, seasickness.

In this chapter the main problems are commented on with advice for their avoidance and, if that fails, some general hints for their treatment.

A first-aid box should be stowed within reach of the cockpit or companionway together with a waterproof torch. The contents of the box, apart from such universal necessities as bandages, absorbent pads of lint, plasters, scissors, et cetera, should be made up from advice given by your local medical source since drugs and, in some cases, treatment, varies quite markedly from country to country. A first-aid booklet should also be included.

Injuries

Bad weather inevitably increases the chances of minor injuries as well as such serious matters as broken limbs. Yet these chances are greatly reduced by seamanlike precautions, many of which need to be taken before even leaving harbour.

Proper stowage of gear and equipment, on deck and below, will prevent many incidents caused by such things as tripping on loose ropes, catching fingers on things out of place, or being hit by hard and nobbly items left lying about.

Inadequate footwear, or none at all, when the feet are not hardened to such treatment, can lead to real pain if a toe is stubbed against a deck bolt or stanchion.

Continuous wetness softens the resistance of the skin, so that unaccustomed hands quickly become sore; often too sore to heave on a rope. Gloves can help those unused to conditions at sea. Plastic gardening gloves are windproof and so are good for helming, but the special fitted gloves made for sailing are better for rope work.

A small point in itself, yet annoying enough to lead to other troubles, is that finger nails also are softened and easily torn. They should therefore be cut short before a sea passage, unless cosmetic considerations are vital, when gloves can be worn.

Those who normally lead a sedentary life are much more liable to injuries than those whose muscles are well exercised and whose limbs are tuned to withstand rubs, bumps and twists. As the season progresses cuts and bruises will become far less frequent.

It is sound seamanship to adapt a voyage to the crew, keeping first to sheltered waters and short hours until all are accustomed to the strains of sailing and living on board a small craft.

4.1 Rough weather can often be exhilarating, but only if the crew are well prepared for it.

4.2 Maintaining one's body in top condition, which means warm, dry and injury-free, starts with proper clothing. Note the two-piece oilskin suit with bib-and-brace trousers, hood, smock top, wrist and ankle bands, neck cloth, wind proof gloves for helming and reinforced fitted gloves for rope handling, and proper short boots.

Burns and blisters

Rough weather is a contributory cause to many of the burns in a boat.

Only hardened seafarers will try much cooking in bad weather at sea, but almost anyone is likely to boil a kettle or saucepan for hot drinks. The dangers are in the spilling of hot liquid from saucepan, kettle or cup, or of grabbing something hot to save oneself

from the results of a lurch or a slip, caused perhaps by something greasy spilled on the floor; fire from spilled fuel or burning fat or oil is also a risk.

Precautions include proper stowage, clean floors and worktops, and fire extinguishers to hand. Another point is that absorbent clothing soaking up spilled hot liquid can even increase burn damage; so perhaps the best first defence is for the cook to

wear at least bib-and-brace oilskin trousers in rough weather which will give excellent protection.

Burns and blisters caused by a rope running fast through the hands, or over bare flesh, can be really painful. This happens most often in rough weather when the strains on ropes are great. The only sure prevention comes from learning how to handle ropes, and this should start in harbour.

4.3 A common cause of head injury is a flying headsail clew or a swinging boom. A runaway halyard will put a hand out of action as will a blow from a spinning winch handle. Burns from spilled hot liquid can be avoided by wearing oilskins.

Seasickness

We are land creatures, tuned to our life on firm ground. The motion of a boat at sea in rough weather upsets this and it is perfectly natural to suffer from seasickness.

There are many stages which may range from a mild feeling of discomfort with disinclination to make an effort, to the extreme of severe nausea accompanied by a complete inability to carry out normal tasks. Very few people are totally immune, although most are less and less affected as they get used to the sea and the boat.

Seasickness should never be treated as a joke; it is one of the most important factors affecting the safety of small craft, and is responsible for the majority of mistakes in rough weather.

Many drugs are available to combat seasickness, and un-doubtedly different people are affected in varying ways; so it is as well to find out which suits an individual best. Some make people drowsy but the question is whether they would be any more effective as crew if miserably seasick. If you do take drugs, make sure you follow the instructions carefully, which usually include the need to take the first dose *before* setting out.

The most vital factor for the skipper is to be fully aware that those who have no recent experience of rough weather in that type of craft are prone to be sufferers. Too much must not be expected of them if it becomes rough, so all possible should be done before getting into the open sea.

Certainly skippers should be on their guard against those who insist 'Of course I'm never seasick', at least until things have been tried out. The need to hang head downwards in the bilges dealing with a fuel leak while the boat is thrown around mercilessly by the seas is a severe test for anyone, while merely going below to fetch a sail will be too much for many people.

There are a few tips which can help in avoiding the worst, or which could delay the onset long enough for the passage to be completed. First, have a good simple meal before setting out; take particular care to dress fully to be warm and dry; when in the cockpit keep occupied if possible. Quite often someone showing early signs of lassitude can be revived to remain a useful crew member by being given the helm or spinnaker sheet.

4.4 The first signs of the onset of seasickness are lassitude and a disinclination to do anything. A wise skipper can often win back a useful crew member by putting him on the helm.

4.5 In a rough sea every job takes far longer and is many times more difficult. Just remaining on board is exhausting enough, without being able to spare a hand and energy to muzzle a thrashing headsail.

Exhaustion

Bad weather is particularly tiring for everyone on board a small craft, whether active or not, as energy is expended just countering the motion when sitting still, while each step takes a great deal more time and effort than in calm conditions.

Almost every job is far harder to do. Lowering and gathering in the headsail might in calm seas be a simple five minute task for a pair of children; yet in rough weather it could mean a twenty minute battle for a couple of strong adults, leaving them gasping and bruised as they crawl back to the cockpit. They will certainly need

ten minutes to recover before bagging up the sail down below. After that it will mean another rest before getting out the chart, laying off a couple of bearings, retrieving the dividers whose points punctured ones foot on the way to the bilges, and deciding on the course to steer.

When a lively boat is sailing fast to windward in brisk conditions she will be pounding into the waves in a way that reminds one of a rat being shaken to death in a terrier's mouth.

Much can be done when cruising to reduce the strain, partly by easing the speed of the boat, and partly by anticipating things so that they can be done before the

motion becomes too bad. Jobs postponed will mean harder work later on if the weather worsens, while exhaustion may lead to a forlorn hope that the job may not need to be done at all if left long enough. A skipper must strive hard to avoid such a doctrine as 'I can always go below and search for the storm jib if it gets rougher; but I can't remember where it is stowed, and it will be such a bother to search for it now'.

So the rule is—Do it now or, do it early!

Seasickness and exhaustion combined can lead to a state of not caring what happens next.

This may deteriorate into wishing only that it would all end and that the waves would swallow one up.

In a small craft it is easy to feel with the seamen of old that Poseidon, ancient god of the seas, is lashing the waves to fury out of spite. An exhausted man huddled in a wave and wind-swept cockpit, peering into the murk, can easily come to imagine the shapes of waves and flying spray turning into sneering laughing faces luring him to some folly. So close to the sea the whistle of wind in the rigging rises to an eerie shriek with the gusts. The alarming crash of a big wave against the hull and the occasional snarl of a breaking top is ever more threatening. By

night conditions seem much worse; this can turn passive anxiety into active fear.

Fear can be a useful protection against danger in a creature's natural environment; but to a land creature at sea it brings additional danger. It may scream at him to run faster from the wind and waves, when such advice is false; or it could yell at him urgently to make for the land, when that might be fatal.

Inspiration and leadership

The skipper has the task of inspiring those on board with the thought that waves in the open sea are dangerous mainly to those who challenge them with speed and impatience. He must strive to make them feel comforted by sea room, and appreciate that approach to the land in rough weather could be hazardous, while it is perfectly safe to ride out the gale by sailing gently or lying hove-to in the open sea.

These thoughts can be strongly aided by seeing that his crew are well fed, warm and rested. In a small craft each of these will have needed planning. Clothing we have mentioned already in this chapter, but the skipper who, before leaving harbour, sees to this and that everyone also has a plastic bag for dry clothing, is on the way to being a leader in rough seas before even going to sea.

Alcohol has for centuries been used to back up courage, both ashore and afloat, sometimes getting its effect by blinding to danger. It is certainly not recommended aboard a small craft in rough weather for this effect, yet it can be a valuable asset when properly used. Particularly it can help those going below after a watch on deck to overcome the insomnia caused by cold feet and hands which is a common feature of bad weather sailing. A tot of

4.6 Proper sea-going bunks will make it possible to sleep in rough conditions. They should be deep and narrow, and fitted with a canvas lee-board. If the bunk is too wide the sleeper will shift with every roll. He must be wedged securely. Nicolson gives dimensions for the minimum size of berth for a full grown man as being 1′ 4″ wide at the head, 1′ 9″ at shoulders and hips, and 1′ 1″ at the foot. If the yacht's side slopes, the widths can be less than this.

spirits for adults will send warmth to the tips of the fingers and the ends of the toes.

Music is another traditional support against fear. When the wind is shrieking through the rigging outside, radio or taped music can give great reassurance to those battened down in the cabin.

The sight of another vessel on a gale driven sea is also comforting, and should one be sighted from on deck, it may be a kindness to tell those down below.

Fortunate is the person who can sleep in a gale. If the bedding is reasonably dry, the berth fitted with a lee board to prevent the potential sleeper being hurled out,

and if he can be wedged in to avoid being thrown up to the deck head, it may be practicable.

Certainly such sleep is invaluable to store up strength against the effort required when conditions improve. It will be a time when full sail needs to be set, the yacht's position re-established, the cabin dried, a hot meal prepared and, no doubt, there will be repairs to be made good on deck and below.

4.7 This happily named yacht is obviously snugged down for a rough passage. She is well reefed and has a small headsail just right for this wind. The crew look happy and relaxed. One must criticize, however, that for a prolonged passage, the reef might be furled more tidily and the dinghy should be more securely lashed.

5 Harbour preparations

The effects of bad weather may well depend on the preparations, or lack of them, which were made when in harbour. Sails, for example, are the essential motive power of a yacht and can stand up to severe strains in a gale at sea if properly used, yet may fail solely due to lack of harbour maintenance.

The old adage 'a stitch in time saves nine' has very real meaning when a few worn stitches ignored in a seam of the mainsail suddenly turn to a split along its whole length as a wave flops into the foot of the sail. Worse still, every stitch sewn aboard a boat tossed by rough seas falls far short of the neat sewing possible when the sun shines down on our boat lying quietly in harbour; and that is even before seasickness is considered.

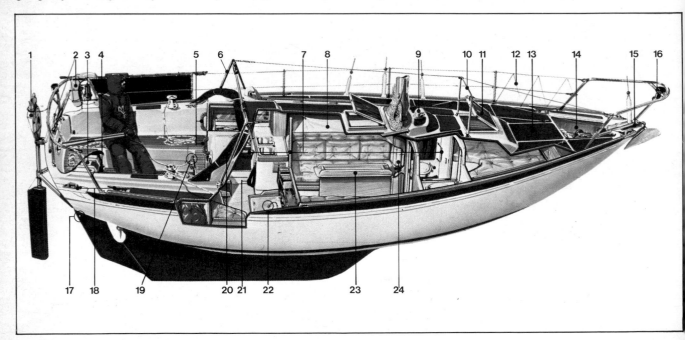

Courtesy—Practical Boat Owner magazine.

5.1. *Key*: The well found yacht;
Desirable features for all-weather passage making.
 1. Self-steering gear
 2. Dan buoy, life buoy and light
 3. Life raft stowage
 4. Large size cockpit drains
 5. Grab handles in cockpit and on deck
 6. Permanent boom gallows
 7. Grab rails near stove and in cabin
 8. Lee cloths on bunks

 9. 'Dorade' type ventilators
10. Safety harness jackstays
11. Watertight forward escape hatch
12. Sail nettings on guard rails
13. Non-slip deck surfaces
14. Anchor well with winch
15. Anchor in ready-use stowage
16. Pulpit reinforcement carrying navigation light.

17. Rudder hole for jury steering
18. Large, well secured cleats and fairleads
19. Harness strong point
20. Spray hood
21. Cook's safety belt
22. Coloured chart table light to preserve night vision
23. Deep fiddles on tables
24. Cabin heater

There are many other things which ought to be checked before setting out on any passage longer than a day's sail. When secure in a marina berth with only the comforting noises of children's chatter and the convivial clink of glasses to be heard around one, it is easy to fall into the trap of not insisting on thorough checks and preparations for sea. 'We must leave now to catch the tide! We can check that when we are on our way'—is all too common a failing to which most of us have at some time succumbed. But it has time and again shown itself to be serious, or at least very frightening, when some small avoidable breakage at sea leads to a train of further failures so that a real emergency has to be faced without proper preparation.

5.1 shows some of the main items to tick off while still secure in harbour. Some of this will come within the realms of fitting out, or even in the original design of the boat.

An example of this is the proper siting of hand rails. Among the major rough weather hazards for someone off watch lying quietly in a lee bunk, is a fellow crew member who has lost his balance and been thrown across the cabin. Hand rails are just as important on deck and, in both cases, must be through-bolted.

5.2 A sudden lurch can easily catapult an off watch man right across the cabin to smash into a sleeper in the lee bunk. Plenty of good strong solidly fixed hand holds are essential, particularly in rough conditions. They should be through-bolted to the structure since they may be asked to take heavy shock loads.

Similarly the safety harness for the cook should be fitted to a really strong eye bolt and secured with heavy carbine hooks.

Standing and running rigging

The fixed rigging should certainly have been carefully checked when fitting out, but it can sustain damage at any time, especially in harbour, and often unsuspected. Visual inspection will show when a rigging screw has been bent, and the time to discover this is when you can still walk to the chandlery for a replacement.

Also vulnerable in harbour are the spreaders, or cross-trees. A careful look aloft by daylight in harbour should disclose anything wrong, such as a missing bolt. Repairs aloft on a rough, dark night at sea when a shroud is found swinging loosely, may be impossible.

Halyards, sheets and other running rigging can be damaged when hauled taut round a bad lead, such as a wire shroud, a guard rail or a twisted lead block, often not noticed in bad weather.

Headsail sheets are particularly vulnerable as they are frequently adjusted under heavy strain. Failure of a jib sheet, if all goes well, need be no more than an exhausting incident; but how much better to change a worn sheet, or to tape round an unprotected split pin, in harbour, than to be dragged from a warm bunk by an emergency call at night.

Failure of a halyard can be particularly troublesome, especially if it leaves no other avail-

5.3 A bosun's chair is a valuable part of the yacht's equipment. Ideally it should have a canvas bag attached ready to take essential tools and small fittings such as shackles, tape and split-pins. When a man is aloft at sea, another should have his whole attention on the halyard winch, with preferably a third to tail. A rope round the mast holds the chair from swinging.

5.4 Roller reefing gear is a simple, safe and effective system for the cruising yachtsman.

Reefing gear

There are three main methods of reefing the mainsail:

a. The reef-point system, which is fast being phased out.

b. Roller reefing, which is simple and easy provided the gear is maintained, but results often in a rather untidy set, and prevents a boom vang being used.

c. Jiffy, slab, or tackle reefing, which is fast and neat for a rather more experienced crew; it is becoming standard on racing cruisers, and will be found on most new boats.

Whatever method is used it is essential to see that everything works before setting out. The tackles and pendants will need to be rove ready to take down the first reef in systems **a** and **c**. Roller reefing needs no preparation other than making sure the winch

able to re-hoist the sails. Note especially the part which runs through the masthead block when the sail is nearly up.

and gear handles are in place, and ready to hand. Many yachts have sailed vast distances with only this simple system which has proved entirely satisfactory with minimum maintenance.

With jiffy reefing it is important to see that the tackles are not tangled and that the sheaves are well oiled.

Deck gear

The lifelines and pulpits back up the need for personal safety harness so both should be checked before going to sea.

Points to note include the pulpit forward and pushpit aft which might be loosened in collision with a wharf or another boat. The height of the lifelines is a compromise between the waist-high guard rails of a big ship and the unavoidable minimum of interference with setting sail. Every inch matters for crew safety, so a lifeline sagging loosely between the stanchions will not give full protection, and may even act as a trip line.

Lifelines usually have rope tensioning lanyards, to break the electrical loop which would otherwise interfere with radio direction finding; these wear out from time to time and certainly need inspection.

For a disabled yacht in rough weather the anchor can be vital, particularly in situations that are

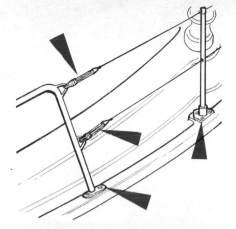

5.5 (Top), Stanchions and pulpits can work loose at the deck mounting plates, or become bent through minor collision. The tensioning lashing works loose and becomes frayed.

5.6 (Middle) An anchor in its ready-to-use position. It can easily be slipped even in very rough conditions and does not have to be carried on a heaving deck.

5.7 (Right), The tender should be very securely lashed down. If it is to double as a life raft some form of slip-knot or easy release clip is essential.

rather desperate and, especially in the dark, that seldom lead to clear thinking. Harbour is the place to ensure that, although properly secured for sea, the anchor can be let go quickly and that its cable will run out from below without jamming; also that it will cease running out before all of it hurtles loose over the side.

The tender

An inflatable dinghy towed astern readily takes off from the water in a strong gust of wind, and before long the painter may part, leaving the dinghy to blow away downwind at speed. A solid dinghy is likely to damage the yacht, or even people in the cockpit, when a following wave carries it into the stern. Its painter too will part in time.

Thus it is best to accept that towing a dinghy on an open sea

passage is an unreasonable risk. It should either be carefully secured on deck, or deflated and stowed down below.

In some small cruisers the dinghy has to double as a liferaft owing to shortage of space. In such a case thought must be given to how to lash it down in a manner whereby it can be released and inflated in a very short time.

Lights, flares, life raft

Collision is a rough weather hazard largely because it is hard to keep a good lookout in bad conditions, when the boat may also be slow to tack or alter course. Thus good navigation lights are particularly important when the weather is bad. Many small yachts seldom cruise at night or use their navigation lights, so a worn out bulb or a defective connection might go unnoticed.

Before going to sea the lights should be switched on to see that they are working correctly. Check also that there is no sign of damage at vulnerable points in the cable, such as where the wiring joins a deck plug. The deck plug should be filled with grease to reduce the chance of salt water getting in and causing a short circuit.

Remember to have a waterproof flashlight handy to the

5.8 At sea in bad weather the tri-colour masthead navigation lights are much easier to see from the deck of a ship than the pulpit type which are frequently obscured by waves or spray. However, maintenance and bulb changing aloft are more difficult and often impossible at sea.

5.9 The life raft must be stowed in such a way that it cannot be damaged and yet can be got overboard without delay. The lifebuoy too should be free in its mounting and ready to be thrown. (see 10.1).

cockpit. This should be checked, and also the spare battery.

When flares or rockets are needed at sea it is usually a matter of urgency, either to warn a ship which insists on closing on a collision course (white flares), or to attract her attention when in distress (red flares).

Before going to sea it should be confirmed that flares are in their correct stowage, within reach of the cockpit, yet where they will keep dry. It should also be checked, from the expiry date printed on each, that pyrotechnics are still within their limit of reliability and that all the crew knows where they are and how to operate them. See

chapter 11 for further information.

A yacht sailing in open waters should have a life raft capable of carrying her entire crew. An inflatable raft designed specially for saving life at sea is particularly suitable and can often be hired for a cruise. It should have a valid certificate to show that it has been inspected and tested within the last year.

Before going to sea the raft should be carefully stowed so that in emergency one person can quickly launch it. This means that it must be secured on deck, or in a locker opening immediately on to the deck.

Engine and battery

The auxiliary engine may have an important part to play in the rough weather handling of a sailing yacht. Just like a human, it too can suffer from its own form of seasickness.

Salt water splashed around is always an enemy of electrics, both owing to its rapid corrosive effect and because it is a conductor. So a boat with the bilges kept dry and the connections well covered in grease is more likely to have an engine that will start in difficult conditions.

The reliability of the engine depends on a constant supply of clean fuel, air and coolant. Unfortunately, the presence of damp and the heavy motion of a yacht in a seaway cause a great deal of trouble and the system needs regular attention.

Necessary checks include the following: water in the fuel will stop a petrol engine and may stop a diesel. Therefore always strain the tank inlet, and check the cap seal; always fit and check a watertrap in the fuel line. Filters should preferably be fitted in pairs so that one can be cleared while the other is in use, and vice versa. Diesels need bleed plugs on the filters too because an air bubble will stop them.

The motion stirs up sediment in the tank. This should be caught by the main filters, if checked and

cleaned frequently, but diesels particularly ought to have at least one back up filter before or after the pump as well. Check that the tank breather is clear or there will be an air lock here and the motor will stop. Spray petrol engine electrics with a water repellent and also check the cooling water inlet since plastic bags are often the cause of a blockage.

Finally check that the right tools are to hand to clean filters at sea and to bleed diesel engine fuel lines.

Many engines cannot be started without a battery so, apart from its other services, it is a special item to check before setting out. It should have a built-in

5.10 Make sure the engine starts first time. So, keep the bilges dry; clamp down the battery under a lid to protect the terminals and electrolyte caps; fit dual filters and keep tools handy for changing them and for bleeding fuel lines.

stowage with a lid and be firmly clamped down. It may have been moved out at some time for topping up or when taken ashore for charging. It is a very heavy object and can do a great deal of damage if it comes adrift. Spilled acid is also very unwelcome in a bilge and, when combined with sea water it makes chlorine gas, which is poisonous.

Stowage

Proper stowage is one of the most important points to take care of in the confined spaces of a yacht and is especially vital if rough weather is expected.

For example, the effectiveness of a bilge pump depends not only upon good design and maintenance, but also upon it getting a fair chance to pump out the water. Should the bilge collect pieces of loose clothing and the packaging of spilled stores, no pump can be expected to cope, even with the aid of a good strum box.

The person who, even in rough seas, carefully stows away wet socks and cardboard cartons so that neither can find their way into the pump suction, is part of the way to being a good sailor. But as we are all creatures of habit, it is best to establish in harbour the practice of stowing everything carefully in its place; then it can be done without conscious effort when the weather is bad.

Epics of improvisation for steering at sea are seldom needed if routine care is taken in harbour. With wheel steering the most likely cause of trouble will be loose gear in the stern locker jamming the quadrant or steering wires. So a harbour check that all is clear, accompanied by an oil can to help any moving parts to run smoothly, is part of rough weather seamanship.

Down below it can be annoying, painful or even dangerous if things are thrown about with the motion of the boat in rough weather. The aim is that before going to sea everything should be securely stowed, and always put back in its place immediately after use. Sometimes it is a three dimensional jigsaw puzzle to work out secure stowage.

Pots, pans and galley knives are among the most painful items to hurtle against a bare arm, a foot or even a face, but the biggest nuisance may be the entire contents of a food locker if it shoots out to land as a mixture of leaking jars, broken bottles, the loose contents of a flour bag, a spilled pepper pot and some soggy packets.

A simple error is to stow all the essential provisions on the same side of the boat. If this happens to be the windward side with the yacht well heeled, no locker lid can be opened without a deluge.

Working tools such as spanners and screwdrivers, or spare winch handles, compete with domestic equipment as bruise makers if left loose on a bunk or the cabin table. An unsecured tool box, with its weight and sharp corners, goes into a higher league of rough weather menaces, as it can even break a limb. Such heavy items should have built-in methods of securing, but failing that they need to be lashed to a table support or some other fixture.

Navigation equipment

It is essential to have the correct charts and guides on board, but it is surprising how often one finds boats without adequate information after they have been recovered from a difficult position. Care must be taken to see that they cover the intended voyage, however short. It is utterly false economy to carry charts just for the start and the destination on the assumption that there is only water in between. That way it is easy in bad weather to get lost in the gap and be quite unable to know when the boat has reached the destination chart. Bad weather may force a yacht to some quite unintended course; so charts must be carried to provide for this.

A boat without an effective compass in rough weather is indeed in trouble also; thus it is wise to carry a second compass and this could be a hand bearing instrument, which is useful in any case for coastal pilotage.

Before leaving harbour it should be checked that the steering compass is in its seagoing position, and that nothing magnetic is stowed too near. Also important is that the deviation card is readily available, and that the compass lighting is in order.

Rough weather clothing

Keeping as warm and dry as possible is vital for maintaining morale and avoiding exhaustion.

So it is important to give careful thought to rough weather clothing before going to sea.

No locker in a small craft is certain to be dry in rough conditions as water from the bilge may run up to leeward behind a bunk. So dry clothing should be sealed in polythene bags for use as required.

Rough Weather Check List

SAILS
Worn seams
Tears

STANDING RIGGING
Loose nuts, bolts, clevis pins, split pins
Missing tape or padding
Loose spreaders
Rigging screws—check for damage or looseness

RUNNING RIGGING
Bad leads
Damaged or seized blocks or sheaves
Worn sheets
Worn or damaged halyards

REEFING GEAR
Check correct operation of roller gear
Reeve pendants and check tackles

DECK GEAR
Pulpit and stanchion bolts
Lifeline lashings
Anchor in ready-use stowage
Cable free to run out
Rig lifelines

TENDER
Dinghy lashed down
Dinghy painter tied to yacht

NAVIGATION
Check correct charts and pilotage guides are on board
Check steering compass and spare, including compass light, deviation card
Check no magnetic gear is close to compass

LIGHTS, SAFETY GEAR
Check navigation lights and wiring
Torch, spare bulbs, batteries
Check flares—type, date and condition
Check liferaft stowage
Check lifebuoy and light
Check crew know how to find and operate all safety equipment
Knife available in the cockpit

ENGINE AND BATTERY
Check fuel, oil, cooling inlet
Note quantity of fuel and range available
Check battery and stowage
Check filters, seals and tank breather
Check tools

STOWAGE
Check lockers in cockpit and cabin
Stow all loose gear or lash down
Screw down jar, bottle and can lids
Secure lids of food packets and galley equipment
Close ports

CLOTHING
Check crew's clothing including plastic bags for spares.

PUMPS
Check bilge pumps
Inspect bilge and strum box
Check canvas or plastic buckets

WATCHKEEPING
Give instructions to crew including details of the planned passage

Getting the best from the crew

Crew organization

The effective strength of a crew depends as much on how it is organized as upon its total number.

When cruising, every person on board should start off with some specific responsibility so as to feel a real member of the crew. Those with limited knowledge must inevitably start with a simple task, yet there should always be something that he or she feels is a personal responsibility.

The skipper can be most effec-tively in command if he has an interested and contented crew, each of whom can contribute something over which he or she has control. Conversely the skip-per who tries to keep everything in his personal charge may in effect turn a boatload of four into a

crew of one, with three incapable passengers. Particularly when it gets rough at sea, such a skipper becomes heavily overburdened. It will then be too late to re-organize, since boredom will have encouraged seasickness, and even mental confusion.

Sharing responsibilities

Whenever a boat is setting out on a voyage which might last more than a few hours, it is a wise skipper who delegates before even leaving harbour. Each member of the crew will have some particular group of tasks and can feel that his or her job is really important for the success of the voyage. Almost certainly the skipper will be able to do most of these tasks much better himself, but it is well worth accepting that things are done slowly when conditions are easy, so as to store up experience and confidence among the crew for when the weather becomes difficult.

One of the skipper's most important functions is to hand out responsibilities suited to the experience, physical strength and

6.1 An interested crew is a happy and efficient crew. The skipper should list the jobs and responsibilities in advance and allocate them, according to ability, for the voyage.

ability of each person. The skipper should also see that each understands how far these responsibilities extend.

One person might have the title of bosun, and many a teenage youngster has proved first rate in this task. It will involve knowing about the sails and rigging, especially where everything is stowed. The bosun should also know where to find the repair equipment.

If such a responsibility can be exercised when conditions are tolerable, it is likely to lead to a determination to know all about that department with a growing proprietary interest in it. The bosun who finds his efforts are respected will have an added incentive to cope with problems, even when tired and feeling sea-sick.

Someone with a mechanical bent could be made responsible for the engine, with the task of knowing how to start, feed and lubricate it, and perhaps also deal with its minor ailments. Electrics could be the same or a separate department, with the need to know how to replace bulbs and fuses, besides seeing that torches have live batteries and are to hand before it gets dark.

Catering is a department, even if each member of the crew plays a part in cooking and washing up. Someone needs to plan the provisions and meals, knowing exactly where everything is stowed.

Either caterer or engineer might be responsible for the fuel supply to the galley stove, but it should be clear in advance whose job it is. If fuel leaks out in rough weather the smell of spilt liquid fuel or leaked gas in a battened cabin may well bring on seasickness.

First aid often goes with the catering, but it should be clear, if someone gets a nasty cut, who it is that can quickly find the first aid box and put on the right dressing.

Navigation is another department, but the skipper may have to retain this as his special responsibility if no-one else knows enough about it. In any case, it is wise to ensure that someone as well as the skipper would be able to find the way to the next harbour.

When a skipper is supported by an experienced crew, he may wish to delegate much of the seamanship and navigation to them. He may get most satisfaction himself by keeping things running smoothly and seeing that all are well fed and comfortable. Thus he might invite his most experienced companion to be navigator and engineer, while the other would be responsible as bosun. The skipper himself might undertake catering and first aid; he will then be in a strong position to deal with important decisions in case of bad weather.

Watchkeeping

Just as the individual crew members are best when organized to have specific responsibilities, so should watches be organized for the best running of the boat. This seems evident, yet so often a yacht gets into difficulties because the skipper sticks to the tiller until utterly exhausted, and is then neither able to continue steering safely, nor to get a watch organization going to relieve him.

There are many different watch systems besides the traditional seafaring method of dividing the crew into two, sharing equal turns of duty on deck and below. In a cruising yacht it is best to work out a system to suit the individualities of the crew, while providing sufficient strength on deck for the job required.

For instance, many a child of twelve years old has proved confident and capable of taking a two hour daylight stint alone at the tiller when conditions are moderate. A pair of such children could together take a four hour watch; but in all cases it is important to nominate who is watch captain giving clear and definite orders.

Typical instructions to the watch captain with a family crew might be to call the skipper immediately in the following circumstances:

—Should a ship be coming

6.2 The watch on deck. Note the life raft at the aft end of the cockpit, and the lifebuoy and floating light ready to hand. Note also that the helmsman is wearing safety harness, though it is not yet clipped on.

towards the yacht
— If a ship comes within one mile
— If the wind increases
— If the sky becomes dark to windward
— On sighting any navigational mark or light
— If in any doubt about anything

Watchkeeping should be an adaptable means of preserving the energy of the crew as a whole, more than a dogmatic regimentation.

Those with natural ability as helmsmen can steer without strain for perhaps six hours, while those for whom it is a conscious effort may find anything more than three hours an ordeal. Bad weather increases the strain of steering, especially if the boat is sailing fast. So in these conditions it would be wise to work short tricks at the tiller or to reduce speed (see chapter 9).

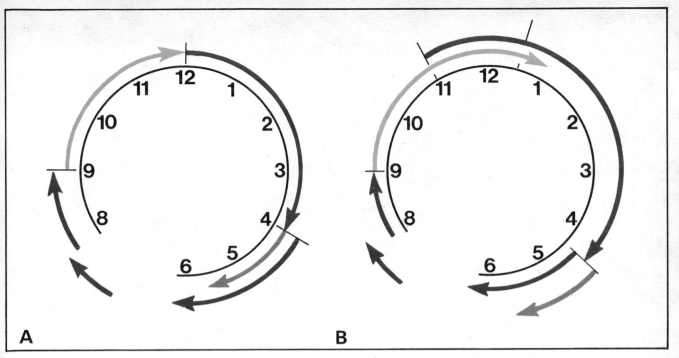

A

B

6.3 A: a possible watch system for fair weather for a crew of two adults and two teenage children. The codes are: dark blue—skipper; light blue—second adult; red—elder teenager; orange—younger teenager. The skipper is always on call and will rest from 4 am and again from 9 pm. Daylight hours are not shown since all the crew will normally be awake.

B: a modification if the weather worsened could include an overlap in the night watches for the two adults as sail is reduced. Then the boat could be hove-to when dawn breaks, so that the skipper can rest. The children would need only to keep a look-out since they would not have to steer or work sails.

Darkness adds further to the strain in bad weather, but much of this is relieved if there is a second person in the cockpit to share the lookout and give support.

The skipper should plan to have his strongest watch-keeping effort during the hours of darkness, particularly around 2 a.m. when everyone is at the lowest ebb. With a family crew this might be done as shown in the diagram on the left. Then should, for example, the weather worsen around 11 p.m. the skipper would be called, when he and the mate would remain on deck until sail had been reduced, after which the mate would go below to sleep.

The skipper would have a fairly long night of it, so with the dawn he might heave-to (see chapter 9). Then, if the visibility is reasonable, the children could safely keep watch, as this would involve no more than one poking a head up the hatch every few minutes for a look out all round.

Heaving-to is specially valuable when much effort has fallen on the skipper, while the rest of the crew is only feeling fit for simple functions, such as lookout duties. Later, when the night watch is rested, sail can be set and the boat got under way again.

75

Safety harness

To give of their best on deck in rough weather, each of the crew must feel secure, and safety harness can provide such security. However, it alarms more than gives assurance if produced for the first time when it is rough; it may even cause obstinate refusal from someone slightly seasick. Indeed, when wearing several jerseys to keep warm, and oilskins on top to keep dry, and with the boat in skittish form, it is thoroughly difficult to get into harness at all.

Safety harness must first be tried on in pleasant conditions when there is plenty of time to make sure it is correctly adjusted and comfortable.

Then it needs to be worn when going about the normal working of the boat in easy conditions, so that the body can become accustomed to the slightly different balance and minor restrictions in movement that it entails.

Practice is needed in the technique of moving forward on deck, and shifting the safety line hook from one anchorage to another. Working on the foredeck with the harness on needs a technique which differs from that when free to move around unhampered. Remember, free to move also means free to be washed overboard and so one should accept the slight restriction that the

6.4 Practice putting on safety harness, and working with it, in calm weather.

6.5 A permanent jack-stay to clip on to is best, but failing that secure yourself to something solid, or even a guardrail.

wearing of safety harness entails, especially in rough conditions.

Keeping dry

The commonest cause of getting wet in worsening conditions is that waterproof clothing is not put on in time. This seems absurd for intelligent human creatures, but bad weather militates against physical and mental effort, so the natural inclination is to wait until a wave splashes over the cockpit before making a move to don waterproof clothing. However, by this time one is soaked!

There is also a reluctance to put on waterproofs down below before going on deck. This is normally due to some degree of seasickness which overcomes common sense.

Rough weather clothing was touched on in chapter 4. The essentials are a good two-piece oilskin with hood, neck cloth, at least two jerseys or an overall insulated inner suit, long johns or thick denim trousers, socks and boots. Plastic gloves are also useful for the cold night watches. Extra dry inner clothes should be ready to hand in a strong plastic bag.

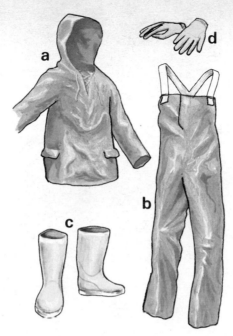

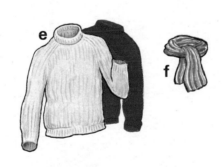

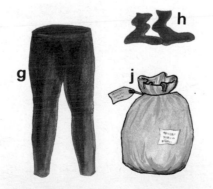

6.6 Minimum clothing for a sea passage: **a**, a good oilskin smock with hood, storm cuffs and neck strap; **b**, high waisted oilskin trousers; **c**, medium length boots with non-slip soles; **d**, plastic gloves; **e**, two jerseys; **f**, neck towel; **g**, long johns or thick denim trousers; **h**, thick socks (oiled seaboot type preferably); **j**, spare set of inner clothing in a plastic bag, labelled and tied.

Food and drink

Rough weather leads to long hours on deck, for which sustenance is important. For instance if the skipper had to be up all night, those going below would probably feel too wet, cold and seasick to find suitable food for passing up to him.

Planning is necessary to ensure that substantial snacks are always available in the cockpit, kept in a waterproof tin or box. Dried fruit is excellent as it is still edible when the sea creeps into the tin, which would make a mush of chocolate for example.

Drink is essential as, strange to say, dehydration is one of the chief effects of life at sea. Racing crews often have a large plastic container of diluted orange juice always in the cockpit in bad weather and at night, and the watch is encouraged to drink. This is a good rule for the family cruise also.

Practice makes it calmer

However simple the equipment, a job like reefing the mainsail for the first time on a dark, wet night is enough to make it seem really rough. Conversely a well practiced crew can make the tempo so much calmer in a rough sea that the waves seem to be quieter as well.

Each member of the crew should become familiar in easy conditions with any task that might come his way in rough. Thus every evolution, such as tacking, gybing, reefing and changing headsails should be practised with the crew changing places, so that each has experience of every job. It is fun in fine weather to see how smoothly the evolutions can be carried through; success in this will take away some of the fears of rough weather.

In the same way, whoever is to take a trick at the steering, should have practice in manoeuvring the boat. When it is rough, or when visibility is bad, another craft might be sighted for the first time very close at hand; so the helmsman needs to be familiar with thë feel and the routine of a quick tack or a gybe.

Sometimes the helmsman of a yacht is too frightened of gybing to consider it a possible manoeuvre for himself, as, in his experience, the skipper has always

6.7 and **6.8** Practise boat-handling routines in fine weather by throwing a lifebuoy overboard and then manoeuvring the yacht to pick it up. Change places so that everyone has a go at each job.

taken over the tiller before a gybe. The helmsman who has never tacked in the dark can lose his sense of direction, either stalling in irons, or swinging the boat too far round to gybe accidentally before adjusting to the new tack. Doing the job even once yourself is a better lesson than seeing it done a hundred times.

The auxiliary engine can be a valuable safety factor in various situations. For example when the wind is so light that a boat scarcely has steerage way as a big ship nears her on a collision course; or again, in a heavy head sea which hinders her from tacking to avoid some hazard.

In such cases the need for the engine is an immediate one; so those actually on deck must be able to start it at once. However simple this may be, the practice of having done it several times is the best safeguard against anyone pressing the wrong knob in an emergency.

The skipper of a lightly manned cruising boat is as likely as anyone else to be washed overboard; indeed, if he has yet to instruct his crew in all the numerous jobs on deck, he is the one who is most likely to be caught off balance or to slip at the wrong moment.

Should this happen his plight is indeed desperate if no-one left on board has ever practised recovery procedure at the tiller. Practising

6.9 It is quite feasible to pick up a swimming man in the bight of a sail. He will be too heavy with water for a weak crew to pull in over the side, but with this method it can be done single-handed. Try it first in fine weather.

in easy conditions with a lifebuoy or empty cardboard box adds interest, and also does much to reassure each member of the crew should rough weather be met.

6.10 Make sure, in fine weather, that you know how the boat reacts when hove-to.

7 Avoiding the worst of the weather

Foreseeing strong winds

Most of the problems of bad weather could easily be dealt with if we always knew what was coming well in advance. So it is important to study the weather carefully to try to anticipate changes, using all the information available.

Radio forecasts are the most important guide, but none should be treated as an oracle. Shipping forecasts normally cover wide areas of sea, but the yachtsman is often fairly close to the land and so may be largely affected by local influences.

The official Met. forecasts are concerned mostly with the gradient wind caused by atmospheric pressure systems, and these will be the prevailing winds in the forecast area. Yet even in the open sea a heavy rain squall may move across the area, carrying a big temporary increase of wind on one side, and an easing of wind on the other. That temporary increase is of little interest to big ships but it could be important to a small sailing craft, especially if it was not seen coming.

In waters within ten miles or so of the coast, a major influence at certain times of the day may be coastal winds caused by temperature differences between land and sea, as air tends to blow from cool areas to hotter. These land and sea breezes are particularly significant in areas such as the Mediterranean, but on hot summer days they also have quite an important influence in cooler climates. Thus when the radio correctly forecasts for the English Channel a steady wind of force 3, if a hot sun has been shining over the land, the afternoon sea breeze might stiffen the breeze locally up to a strong force 5 or more.

This sea breeze will also make a lee shore for a yacht approaching the coast, but danger can be avoided by planning arrival for early morning or late evening when the sea breeze will not be operating.

There are so many individual possibilities when trying to forecast the approach of bad weather that the skipper ought to study text books on the subject. However a few typical cases, mainly for temperate latitudes, can be given and also some signs of local disturbances which would affect a yacht.

Approaching front or depression

The typical sign of deterioration in a spell of fine weather is a veiling of the sun by flat featureless high clouds. Lower clouds will still be present but will decline. Low grey cloud will build up again later bringing rain and wind. So the crew of a yacht can expect poor visibility, rain and winds which veer as the fronts pass through in the northern hemisphere; thus they back in the southern hemisphere.

The strength of the wind depends to a great extent on the depression itself. Some indication will be given in radio forecasts but winds could be a great deal stronger in coastal areas. Sometimes a second depression closely follows the first and often brings even stronger winds.

Approaching strong wind

Typical signs are high cirrus clouds in parallel bands or streaks, usually from the north-west in the northern hemisphere or from south-west in the southern hemisphere. Low cumulus clouds pass from left to right (northern hemisphere) when facing the apparently converging streaks of upper cirrus, which warns that strong to gale winds can be expected in a few hours. During this

7.1 The approach of a depression after a period of fine weather can be signalled by a gradual veiling of the sun by fairly featureless high cloud. The cumulus underneath will die away, as here, before being replaced by grey overcast and rain.

7.2 The barometer may not fall very fast on the approach of even a deep depression, as is shown by these traces. It depends partly on where you are in relation to the line of approach. The red lines indicate the upper air stream which carries the advance warning cirrus cloud.

7.3 Cirrus streaks in parallel bands warn of strong to gale winds to come. Low cloud moves from left to right here and this is also the quarter where the wind will be later.

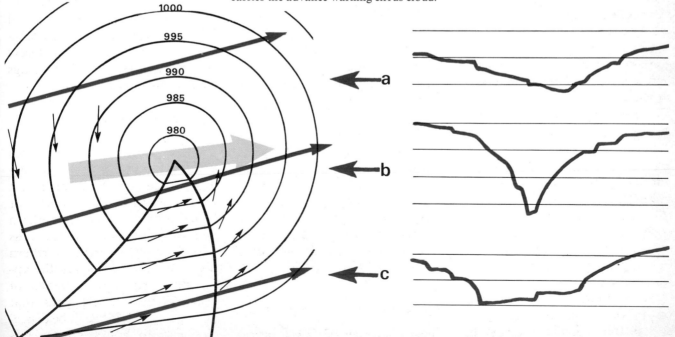

period cloud will form lower down and will cover the sky and bring rain and increasing wind.

Windshifts and change to squally weather

After a period of solid continuous rain and low cloud with fresh winds, the sky may show through in patches or suddenly clear almost completely. This marks the passage of a cold front and heralds the final phase of a depression.

Winds will veer immediately, sometimes very sharply up to fifty or sixty degrees. The air stream is now unstable and winds will be squally. Warning of squalls will be given by the approach of a heavy build-up of dark based clouds. (*7.5* and *7.6*).

Line squalls

There is a type of fierce wind which needs alertness on deck to anticipate it since the yacht's barometer is unlikely to give any warning. This is the line squall which occurs in any of the temperate regions of the westerlies, and also sometimes in the tropical zones of the Horse Latitudes. Its coming can usually be spotted when, with a clear sky overhead, a long line of low black cloud is seen approaching, while beyond it is a uniform light grey sky.

As the line of black cloud gets nearer, it usually appears roll

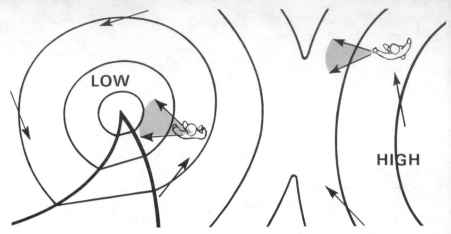

7.4 The rule in the northern hemisphere is that, if you stand with your back to the wind, low pressure will be on your left. Face the wind in the southern hemisphere. The forecast may give the direction of advance of the low area so that the position of its centre can be estimated.

7.5 The typical hard leading edge of a line squall, which sometimes reaches from horizon to horizon. The violent wind and rain can be seen beginning near sea level.

shaped and threatening. In the northern hemisphere the wind typically falls light from the south until the edge of the dark cloud is nearly overhead. Then a violent squall pipes up from the north west, often reaching gale force. In the southern hemisphere the wind falls light from the north, and the squall hits from the south-west.

These line squalls are common in the Mediterranean and around the coasts of Europe and North America. Off the coast of South America they are known as the Pampero, while off South Australia they care called Southerly Busters; they are also frequent off South Africa.

When air masses come quite dry from the Sahara, cloudless line squalls sometimes hit the Mediterranean waters and are then known as white squalls. An alert watch on deck should be able to hear the wind coming, and sometimes a line of white breaking sea may be seen in time to get all sails down and secured. This would usually be the safest tactic as the white squall seldom lasts long enough for a sea to build up.

Thunderstorms

Often a light wind drifting towards the storm is suddenly converted into a very strong gust away from it accompanied by hail, rain and almost nil visibility. If it looks threatening all sails should be taken off the yacht and lashed down.

Most bad weather will be due to the change in pressure due to the movement of large scale weather systems. To anticipate these, the best guide is regular attention to the shipping forecasts. A series received about every six hours will give a much better sense for the weather than a single forecast but, owing to their necessarily general nature, one should also keep notes of the yacht's own barometer readings. These should show the local trend much more precisely and enable the navigator to estimate the time of arrival of a front or weather system.

With enough experience the appearance of the clouds can be read almost like a book, while a shift in wind direction, a drop in temperature, or the arrival of a long swell all have their messages to interpret. A skipper could well go below for a sleep with an easy mind, his boat sailing quietly over a calm sea in a gentle wind. But he would surely be unhappy if he came on deck six hours later to find that those on watch had hardly noticed that the wind had backed and that banks of low cloud were forming to windward.

7.6 An approaching squall, which may range from an isolated patch of wind of short duration to a full-blooded thunderstorm lasting an hour, is signalled by dark clouds.

Use of the auxiliary engine

Good seamanship demands the best use of whatever equipment is available, so the auxiliary engine of a sailing cruiser can be valuable in helping to avoid bad weather, even if it has limited use once the conditions are really bad.

For instance, if the skipper on looking out of the hatch realizes that a front is approaching, he might assess that within four or five hours it would be cold, raining and steadily getting rougher.

Perhaps there is a harbour with a safe approach twenty miles away. With the yacht sailing close-hauled and with four hours of favourable tide, she could just point for it at first; but the increasing wind would mean reducing sail and, with the rougher seas, she would make more leeway and be well to leeward of the harbour when the tide turns. With a good engine a sound plan would be to start it at once to make the best speed to windward in conjunction with the sails, while the conditions are still moderate. Without loss of speed, sail could be reduced while work on deck is still relatively easy.

The extra speed would still give a better chance of making a landfall to establish the position before the rain reduced visibility; while the snug rig, assisted by the engine, would perhaps enable her to reach the harbour on one tack,

7.7 The boat travels well to windward with a reefed mainsail to steady her and provide some power, with the engine pushing her through the wave crests.

saving several hours of beating against tide and wind in rough seas.

It is unlikely that a sailing yacht's auxiliary engine will be powerful enough to push her to windward in the open sea once the waves have built up under a fresh to strong breeze. Yet if such a wind is expected, the engine can back up the sails in gaining a few miles extra to windward before it comes on to blow.

Should a yacht have the misfortune to lose her mast, and is able to clear it all away, the engine will be more effective to windward than when pushing against the windage of the rig as well.

Whenever using the engine in rough seas, special care must be taken that a rope's end is not washed over the side, where it could catch in the propeller and put the engine out of action.

7.8 (Upper, right) The windage of the hull and rig, and the smashing of the wave crests against the bow mean that she can hardly make progress to windward under reduced sail alone.

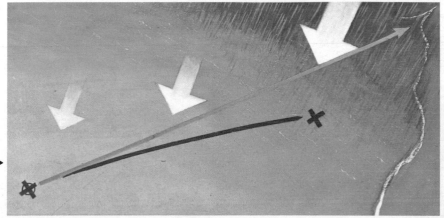

7.9 With power-assisted-sail the yacht reaches harbour before the worst weather arrives. Under sail alone she sags to leeward of her course, the tide turns against her and rain blots out the land.

The turn of the tide

One factor affecting rough seas that can be foretold with reasonable accuracy is the change of tidal streams. We have seen in chapter 1 that the wind blowing over a contrary stream builds up the sea whereas, when the tide turns to run in the same direction as the wind, the sea will go down.

Take the case of a yacht sailing quietly with a forecast of no change in weather, a strong tidal stream in her favour, and the destination thirty miles away. She might expect no difficulty before reaching harbour in daylight some six hours later.

With a fair stream setting at $2\frac{1}{2}$ kts., and the boat sailing through the water at $5\frac{1}{2}$ kts. (left, in *7.10*), she will be making good a speed over the sea bottom of 8 kts. The apparent wind she feels is a modest 10 kts.; yet the true wind, such as would be felt by a moored lobster pot buoy, would actually be a moderate breeze of 18 kts., or a good force 5. Remember that her own and the current's speed are added to the wind felt on board to arrive at the true wind speed.

The tidal stream turns three hours later and, as it increases to its full strength in the opposite direction, an entirely different situation develops, although the true wind has not altered at all and the boat's speed through the water is the same. The stream will

then be struggling at $2\frac{1}{2}$ kts. against the 18 kt. wind (right, in *7.10*) making the sea quite rough with steep waves.

The yacht will now only be making good a speed of $3\frac{1}{2}$ kts. over the sea bottom ($5\frac{1}{2}$ minus $2\frac{1}{2}$) so the wind felt in the sails will have gone up from 10 to 15 kts. This increased apparent wind, combined with the rough sea, will make the boat harder to handle,

with more chance of little things going wrong.

Difficult to steer, and with the tide against her, she probably will not reach harbour before dark after all, while her crew will protest that the forecast failed to warn of a substantial increase of wind and sea!

Much of the trouble could have been avoided if the tidal changes had been anticipated. Just at the

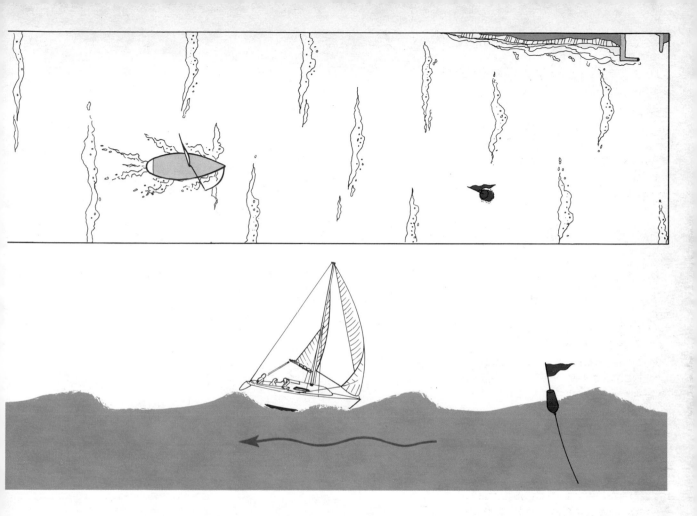

time the tidal stream turned, waterproof clothing and safety harness could have been put on and then sail reduced. With the increase in apparent wind the boat would sail just as fast with less sail, and would be easier to steer and more comfortable. Just as important, the crew would be at ease with the true knowledge of what was happening, instead of apprehensive about the worsening conditions.

Remember that the speed of a yacht is so low that the speed of the tidal stream is of great importance in planning even the shortest of passages. Tide tables should always be consulted before setting out and extract notes made of the strength and direction of the stream for a period of at least half as long as the trip is expected to last.

7.10 There is no change in the true wind speed between the two parts of the drawings, at left and right. However the tide has turned and this has caused a dramatic alteration in the sailing conditions.

By-passing a race

When bad weather threatens there is a natural inclination to cut corners fine when making for shelter, with the understandable feeling that a mile or two saved could make all the difference. This is especially so when the speed of the boat through the water is perhaps six knots, or even much less over the ground when a contrary tidal stream or current is running fast. A saving of two miles might then represent at least an hour in time.

Yet this corner cutting is sometimes the reason for a yacht sailing into the really rough seas that can occur off a headland and perhaps getting into serious trouble. This is true whether it is in tidal waters or in the relatively tideless seas where the currents are caused by prevailing winds.

Such rough areas near a headland, or over an underwater ledge are made worse should a strong wind blow against the general movement of water. The greater turbulence may lead to a really dangerous rough and tumble where a boat could be pooped, swamped or badly knocked about by steep breaking waves or overfalls.

When the race is mainly due to a tidal effect, its position in relation to the land will often move at different states of the tide. At slack tide there will often be no race at all, but this may last for perhaps only fifteen minutes and a boat already in the area may suddenly find the water around it starting to 'boil' for no immediately apparent reason.

To show the true extent of the problem, take the case of a yacht making for the imaginary Haven Harbour from the west in threatening weather. From her present position, and steering to pass half a mile off Sharp Point, she would have ten miles to go over the sea bottom.

With a south-westerly wind let us assume that she can sail at $5\frac{1}{2}$ kts. through the water on both legs of her track, and that the tidal stream or current is setting against her at a good 3 kts. off Sharp Point, easing to 1 kt. in her present position and also when once round the corner. Allowing for this contrary set, she should near the harbour entrance in about three hours time.

The wise seaman would in this case lay off a course to pass well off Sharp Point because, even without local knowledge, it will obviously be a dangerously rough area. She should then hold on until comfortably past the race before turning across the tidal stream for Haven Harbour.

A course set to pass two and a half miles out would add some four miles to the distance over the ground, but the contrary stream

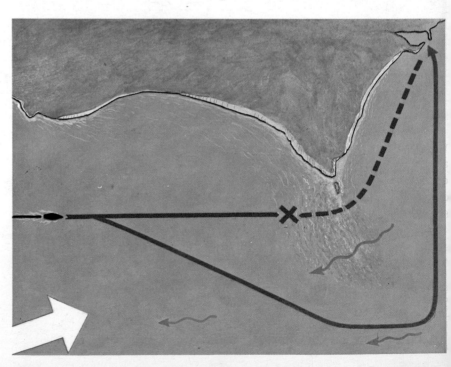

would not be as strong out there as it will be close to the point. So on distance and tidal stream calculations alone she might take something under an hour more than on the shorter corner-cutting course. Yet the effects of the turbulent race, taking the inner track, would most probably lead to problems that would slow her down more than that, and could be perhaps dangerous as well.

Though we are thinking in this example of a current against a yacht, a race can be just as dangerous when the current is favourable. The yacht would be swept through it in a short time but it

7.11 A race should always be avoided where possible even if it adds an hour or so to the length of the passage. For the experienced skipper there is sometimes justification in attempting to pass close in at the turn of the tide when the race ceases temporarily, but this will entail arriving at precisely the right time.

7.12 Even on this calm day, on an apparently open sea, there is broken water and overfalls in the area of this race. In rough weather this area would be dangerous for a small boat.

only needs one awkward wave to do the damage.

Keeping clear of a lee shore

We have seen in chapter 1 how the seas off a lee shore are usually rougher than in open water well clear of the coast. If the coast is steep and rocky, with deep water up to the foot of the cliffs, waves may be reflected back to mount up as they meet the incoming waves, creating confused and steep seas. However, this is seldom significant as much as half a mile out from the cliffs, so it can readily be avoided by keeping a reasonable distance off the coast.

A problem comes when the destination is a harbour on a lee shore. The experienced seaman knows when conditions make it hazardous to approach such a harbour, but sometimes he is forced to attempt the risk of running for shelter in doubtful conditions, and even he may get into trouble.

The seaman with less experience of that particular harbour approach must obviously be more careful. If he is in any doubt, he should either stay at sea until conditions moderate, or make for some other harbour whose approach is less exposed—best of all one on a weather shore.

The shoaling lee shore is normally a greater hazard than the steep-to rocky coast, as the danger is less obvious. Chapter 1 described the effect of shoaling on open water seas and showed how the waves steepen and break at a certain stage. Low lying coasts with shoals extending far out to seawards are especially dangerous as navigation is often difficult; a close watch must then be kept on the soundings. Another point is that the approach may look perfectly possible from seawards because the crew are only seeing the comparatively smooth backs of the waves; yet closer in the wave crests breaking down their faces will show that it is too late to turn back.

There is danger in approaching a lee shore in uncertain visibility, but even in clear weather it is important to keep a careful track

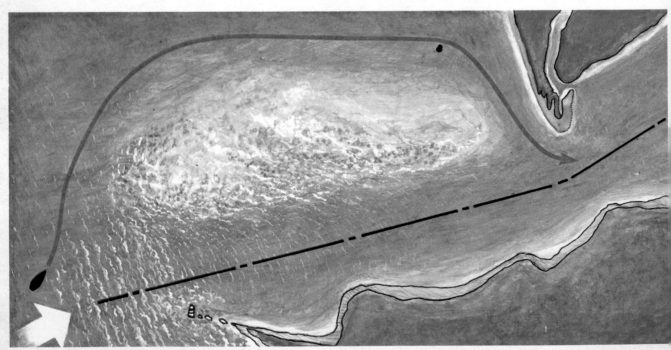

of the yacht's position, making
full use of lightships, buoys and
beacons, when shoals extend
some distance from land. Even
when the position is precisely
known and the weather is clear,
the approach to a harbour on a lee
shore may be dangerous at certain
stages of the tide when the sea
breaks right across the main channel. Sometimes the height of the
tide is critical and when it reaches
a certain level, the seas no longer
break in the channel. Conversely,
on a falling tide there will come a

time when waves which were
previously running quietly into
the entrance, suddenly begin to
break. Sometimes fishing craft are
seen hanging about outside a
harbour; the crews know the
approaches and have decided to
remain well out, making a safe
approach wnen the tide is near its
top, but still rising.

In other cases there are alternative channels, and with a particular direction of wind and sea it
may be possible to select a channel where the approach to shallow
water is sheltered. A good example of this is the western approach
to the Solent where, in a strong
south-westerly wind, the Needles
Channel can be thoroughly

7.14 A coast with shallow waters extending some distance offshore will become
quite impossible for a small yacht to
negotiate. Further offshore in the same
wind, the seas will be much kinder and
may not even break.

rough. In these conditions a yacht
could take a course northwards of
the Shingles Bank, and enter by
the North Channel, which would
be protected by the shoals to
windward.

7.13 A good example of how a detour
would enable harbour to be gained even
in bad conditions. This situation is typical
of the Needles Channel approaches to the
Solent in the prevailing south-westerlies.

8 Gale warning at sea

8.1 Many harbours show warning signals of various types when a gale is imminent. The local coastal pilots and almanacs give the details.

A true gale starts only when force 8 is reached, which will mean winds of 34 to 40 knots average, with gusts often much higher. Though a well found yacht manned by a crew who have taken note of the advice on preparation for hard winds given earlier, should be able to cope, most would prefer to avoid a gale at sea.

There are many clues to an approaching gale and the alert seaman will keep in mind all possibilities.

1. You hear it mentioned or forecast on the radio.
2. You see warning signals ashore.
3. You read a weather report on a boat centre or marina notice board.
4. You notice a change in the barometer.
5. You see typical signs in the sky.
6. It is already blowing hard and looks threatening.

Let us take these in turn:

1. In most maritime countries regular forecasts for coastal shipping are given both on the normal domestic broadcast wavelengths and also on special medium wave, VHF and UHF frequencies. Details are given in nautical almanacs.

It should be regular routine to listen to the shipping forecasts and note down pressures, trends and expected winds. In some areas special pads are available for the more rapid collection of this information. A tape recorder is valuable to record the message which can be transcribed at leisure later, especially as interruptions may occur during the actual broadcast.

Gale warnings, are often broadcast on domestic radio programmes as soon as they are received and are repeated hourly thereafter.

2. Storm signal stations on many coasts show visual signals when there is a local gale or strong wind warning; they consist of cone shapes or flags hoisted on a prominent mast by day, and a corresponding arrangement of lights by night. The skipper should be certain that he checks from local pilotage guides the signals for his particular area.

3. Most boating centres, coastal marinas and many yacht clubs post summaries of the latest weather bulletins on their notice boards. In many places there is a phone number which can be dialled to hear a recording of the local forecast, while it is often possible to speak by phone direct to the actual forecaster in the nearest Met. office.

4. The barometer of itself will not always warn of a gale coming, since the speed at which the weather system moves may control whether it shows a rapid or moderate change. However, here are a few combinations which usually herald a gale:—

A rapid fall combined with a backing of the wind may turn to a gale from south-westwards in the northern hemisphere, or a veering wind may bring a gale

from north-westwards in the southern hemisphere.

A rapid rise and a veering wind may bring a north-west gale in the northern hemisphere. A rapid rise and a backing wind may bring a south-west gale in the southern hemisphere.

5. The two main early warning signs in the sky are a veiling of the sun by a thin featureless high cloud which should give something of the order of six hours notice; while high altitude cirrus streaks may give somewhat longer.

Other signs are the sun setting above a bank of cloud, though this only heralds a depression and not necessarily a gale.

6. If it is already blowing hard, and cloud is lowering and thickening, expect more wind still.

Strong wind with a high barometer may blow from a clear sky but it usually becomes hazy, and

8.2 Even with land close to windward, a mistral can be thoroughly unpleasant for a small yacht.

finally visibility may be of the order of a mile only. This sort of gale from the south to east or north-east quadrants is often a feature of the northern part of a depression in the northern hemisphere, or the reverse in the southern part of a depression in the southern hemisphere.

At sea—making a plan

Important to the yacht is how soon the gale may be expected and the direction from which it will blow. The direction is likely to be correctly forecast in the radio warning, but the time factor is much more difficult to assess as weather systems are inclined to speed up or check their pace unpredictably.

When a radio message states 'imminent', this implies within six hours; 'soon' is expected within six to twelve hours, while 'later' forecasts longer notice than this.

Careful consideration should be given to the overall situation so that a soundly based plan can be made. Factors to be taken into account include:
— Any navigational hazards such as a lee shore or shoals.
— The ability of the yacht herself.
— The strength and morale of the crew.
— The accuracy of the plotted

position.
— The position of possible shelter within reach.

Normally the nearest shelter, judged by the time needed to reach it, will be to leeward but it may be safest to take the longer course of going somewhere to windward, or which will be to windward after the expected wind shift associated with the approaching fronts. This would then be a weather shore, the sea will be less severe, and harbour approaches easier.

8.3 A typical small but deep summer depression is rapidly moving in from the south-west and, since it formed recently, warning has only just been received by yachts in positions **a**, **b**, **c** and **d**. The depression is fast moving at 30 knots and so there is little time, particularly for yachts **a** and **b** to make a plan or run for shelter.

The depression is 75 miles SW of Harbour E at 0900 and the centre is expected to pass inland over Harbour K around 1900 the same evening, with winds up to force 8 and stronger gusts. Very rough steep seas are forecast, especially just after the centre has passed when the winds in that area will switch rapidly from the south to south-west quadrant towards north-west to north. Visibility will be very poor with heavy rain for a period of three to four hours in most of the coastal area followed by brighter but very squally conditions.

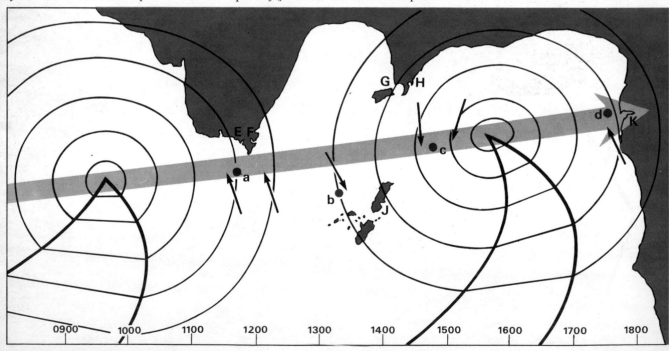

There may be difficulty in this plan because it will not be known at this stage whether the boat and crew will be capable of continuing sailing during the onset of the gale. It may be necessary to heave-to. However, even if the windward refuge is not reached before having to do this, the boat will still have made that much more sea room between it and the lee shore.

If the skipper decides to go for shelter to leeward, he must try to ensure that he will make it in time.

If he fails, he will be faced with having to claw off a lee shore in the teeth of a gale to gain sea room. The crew and the yacht may not be capable of doing this at that stage and they would then be in serious danger.

If the yacht's position is not accurately known the safest course is to gain distance to windward as quickly as possible, using the motor if necessary, then heave-to.

There is an additional risk in

making for a strange harbour in worsening weather, whether it be to leeward or windward. One may find that the only berth available is a partly exposed anchorage or that the channel is too shallow until the tide comes up so that for several hours the yacht must wait outside which, in the case of a refuge to leeward, would be the worst position of all.

8.4 Yacht **a** has a comparatively easy problem even though her warning has been short. The storm centre will pass over her position when the wind will switch from south to north or north-west. She can take routes 1 or 2. Both will mean she is close-hauled after the wind change, but the former course will give her an increasing lee for the last three hours or so. The approach to Harbour F will be dead to windward however, whereas Harbour E entrance will be a reach in, but has a breaking bar at some tide states.

8.5 Yacht **b** might consider making Harbour J after standing off until the wind change when the centre passes—track 1. However the approaches are rock strewn with very strong currents and so the temptation should be resisted. Better to make sea room to the north-west and then heave-to until conditions improve—track 2.

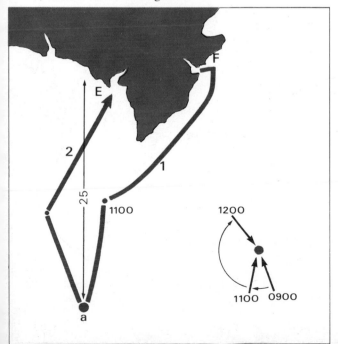

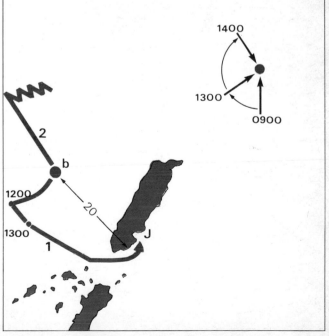

Gaining sea room

When there is no reasonable shelter within reach it is important to have enough sea room to give choice of action. A yacht disabled and then drifting before a gale for six hours would find even twelve miles of sea room scarcely enough for comfort.

When a yacht cruising along a coast with no harbour nearby receives a gale warning it is a sound decision to tack out to sea, gaining distance from the rocky cliffs or shoals. If conditions are still reasonable she can sail at her best speed directly out from the land. However, if the weather is already deteriorating it would be well to bring her down to a snug rig, while work on deck is relatively easy and the crew is still feeling capable of making the effort; then the boat can be steered the course to seawards on which she rides most comfortably.

The average crew of a small cruising yacht will probably feel rather unhappy about sailing out from the land when a gale is forecast, and there will be temptation to run off to leeward, hoping to find shelter eventually.

A gale can be truly diabolical if it strikes a boat close to unseen rocks or shoals, with the crew strength seriously impaired by

8.6 For yacht **c** the temptation is to run for the nearest shelter, which is Harbour H—track 1, but she would only just reach the entrance by the time the centre passed very close by with its violent switch of wind and very poor visibility. Much better to heave-to until after the centre has passed and the visibility improves. Then, in better conditions, and with an increasing lee as she closes the coast, shelter can be reached at H or at Anchorage G.

8.7 With 8 hours to go before the centre passes, boat **d** might go for Harbour K which would be somewhat to windward when the depression's influence comes to be felt. But the last part of the approach would be in very strong and increasing winds with deteriorating visibility. The entrance is also tricky. Better to go southwest as fast as possible and then heave-to during the worst weather.

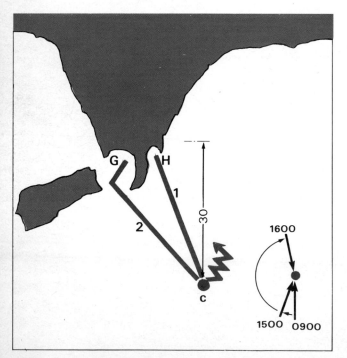

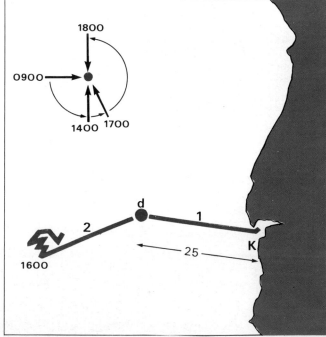

seasickness, exhaustion and anxiety. Then even a minor failure of gear or small mistake in navigation could turn to disaster. Yet, if snugged down, and perhaps twenty miles from any land or shoal, a gale is nothing terrible. It can be a stimulating experience to watch great waves mounting up and the yacht riding to them bravely.

Securing for a gale

By the time it is appreciated that a gale is on the way the weather conditions may be such that there is a strong reluctance to do anything other than sit, steer and perhaps pray. But the skipper must have the determination to take the opportunity to check that all is ready before things get a good deal worse.

This is a situation where previous delegation of the departmental responsibilities will pay good dividends. For example, when someone has grown accustomed to his responsibilities as bosun this will have developed a strong inclination to check that all is well with the rigging. Yet the same person, feeling that he is just one of the crew with no special responsibilities, would lack the motivation to make an effort when feeling wet, tired and slightly seasick.

On deck, things of minor significance when the weather is calm, can become matters of real importance in rough seas. For example, halyard tails left bunched around the foot of the mast would cause no trouble until a wave washes over the deck and turns them into a tangled mass of rope. Then no sail can be lowered or reefed without lengthy sorting out and untangling. This will be much harder if the yacht is by then heeling too heavily and sailing too fast.

If anything on deck, such as a dinghy, an inflatable liferaft, or an

8.8 On coasts with shallow, shelving beaches the harbour approaches are often across a bar and between narrow entrances formed by moles. Impossible in fresh onshore winds!

outboard motor in its deck storage, is just the slightest bit loose, a rough sea will soon get to it and make it looser still. Re-securing such things on deck may be a wet job, but will prevent the nightmare problem of going out on deck in really bad conditions to try and tame a heavy object which seems determined to escape over the side after first bashing anyone who tries to stop it.

This is also the time to ensure that heavy weather sails, such as a spitfire jib, or a storm trisail, are in their correct seagoing stowage. Gear which at the time seems unlikely to be needed, can readily get moved; perhaps the person moving it does not even know what it is, but feels that its position would make a handy stowage for something else. Should the need arise for shifting storm sails, it will be rough enough to make 'hide and seek' through the lockers thoroughly unattractive.

Where the mainsail is reduced by reef points, this is the time to rig the reefing gear.

This will involve working near the outer end of the main boom, which will need to be hauled in within reach of the deck. If the wind is already fresh this will tend to make the yacht heel heavily. It is best to do it before the wind has reached this strength but, if it is too late, then the main halyard can be lowered a foot or two so as to spill some wind out of the sail.

Towed dinghy

An inflatable dinghy is by far the commonest tender to a small cruising yacht. In quiet conditions it is occasionally towed astern on short sea passages but this is not recommended in the open sea. If rough weather threatens at sea the yacht should be hove-to and the dinghy hoisted aboard, then deflated, folded up and stowed below; but much better—do it before leaving harbour.

A solid dinghy, too heavy to hoist aboard, is indeed a risk in gale conditions. The tow rope can be duplicated to reduce possibility of loss, but the greatest danger is that it will be thrown against the yacht to damage gear or injure those on deck. Towing a rope from the dinghy will lessen the chance of this happening, while the tow line itself should be lengthened to put the dinghy well astern.

Securing below

If time and circumstances allow, it will be worthwhile to confirm the harbour checks described in chapter 5.

It is certainly important to confirm that the bilges are as dry as they can be, noting particularly that the pump suction is clear. Also check that all lockers are properly closed; perhaps a food packet stuffed in may be jamming a locker lid shut but preventing the catch from closing. A sudden lurch could lead to a deluge onto the cabin floor, but this can be prevented by a methodical check of each locker, perhaps taking only a few seconds.

Skylights, portlights and the forehatch should be checked as fully shut, in that any one of them could have been temporarily opened since leaving harbour.

Worsening weather is a good occasion to give the auxiliary engine a run. This will increase the chance of starting it without trouble should it be needed later on. It will also bring the batteries up to full charge to keep the navigation lights bright for the night ahead.

All these tasks should be part of the specific jobs of each member of the crew. They are important to ensure the yacht is well prepared but, it is just as vital that such jobs help psychologically to overcome the fear of a coming gale. Someone busy with tasks he knows to be his own responsibility is less prone to anxiety than one who feels powerless to do anything about a frightening experience ahead; he is also less likely to feel seasick.

Good clothing is, of course, essential as we have previously seen. Additionally, however, in a small craft being thrown about violently by the waves, no foul weather clothing is actually easy to put on, although some can be very much better than others. So the skipper must make sure that the crew are either fully dressed before it gets too rough or are given enough extra time to get dressed before coming on deck. So often people get wet unnecessarily by delaying putting on their oilskins. Thus a gale warning is a good time for reminding everyone of the folly of such laziness.

The aim of the skipper should be that all his crew is as ready as possible to carry out their part in handling the yacht when the rough weather comes.

Securing in harbour

Assuming the yacht can reach comparative shelter, perhaps secured at an open mooring, or riding to her own anchor, there will be a number of essential precautions to take.

If on an open mooring:
—Double up the lines to the buoy.
—Wrap anti-chafe cloths where the lines pass the bow fairlead.
—Make sure the lines can be slipped in emergency.
—Have the anchor ready to drop in emergency.
—Lash down any loose gear.
—Rig and furl a double-reefed mainsail and a small jib.

—Start and run the engine to charge the battery.

If lying to the yacht's own anchor, most of the above also apply and in addition the following:
—Get the second anchor ready to drop.
—Estimate from wind direction and tidal predictions how the yacht will lie in relation to the anchor. Will she have enough room to swing? Is there enough room to leeward if she has to get underway or if she drags?
—Ease out more anchor warp (rode) and add chain or a weight to reduce snubbing (see next chapter).
—Take cross bearings from fixed objects as a check against dragging.

During the gale, one person should always be on watch. The watch keeper should look out of the hatch from time to time, occasionally take bearings, check the anchor lines for wear, check the weather by observation and from the forecasts, and generally make sure everything is ready for an emergency.

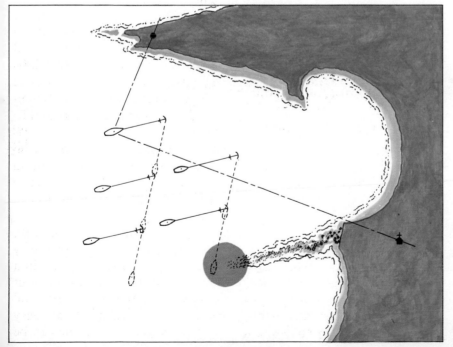

8.9 The yachts in the anchorage will all swing together in a strong wind, so the radii from their anchors can be long enough if care is exercised. Think where the boat will lie when the wind changes. Remember to fix the yacht's position with cross bearings and check them constantly to discover if the anchor is dragging.

Handling in rough weather

The behaviour of a yacht in rough seas will depend much upon skill in steering. An experienced helmsman, in sympathy with the movement of the boat and the seas, will be able to keep her going with reasonable comfort in conditions when the craft would be battered and liable to damage in the hands of someone less skilled.

In rough conditions, the helmsman needs to keep a careful eye on the seas to windward, and to be alert for the extra big wave, or the wave coming from a different direction. If he is able to spot it in time he will then be able to take avoiding action and reduce its shock effect on the hull and crew.

To the experienced man, all of this will be automatic, but the beginner would particularly need to concentrate on his steering, as it will be a wet ride if his mind wanders to other things.

The rough weather helmsman needs to feel comfortable and relaxed. His clothing and oilskins must fit well and keep him warm; his safety harness must make him feel safe, yet not restrict his movement. He should have a firm seating position to windward, so that he gets a good view of the oncoming waves, and is not thrown off balance as the boat lurches.

The change-over of helmsman is a vulnerable time for a knockdown or a broach. The oncoming helmsman should allow a minute or two to sit beside the offgoing helmsman to get used to the feel of the boat before taking over. The inexperienced may need several minutes before gaining confidence.

A tired helmsman is liable to have trouble, particularly if something is disturbing him. For instance the lazy relief who comes on deck after the agreed time for the turnover may cause resentment, and this could lead to a ton of water in the cockpit.

Since good helmsmanship is needed in bad weather to keep the yacht going at its best speed, so in a cruising yacht there is often a tendency for the skipper to stick to the tiller himself, especially if no-one else on board has much experience of such conditions. This could well be acceptable if reliable shelter is near at hand, say within four or five hours sailing, but when there is a probability of having to stick it out much longer it is important that the skipper should preserve his energies for future demands. The less experienced his crew is, the more necessary is it that he staves off the exhaustion which could undermine the quality of his decisions. The solution is to make it easier for the less experienced helmsman, which can be done by reducing sail, or even to make no helmsman necessary by heaving-to.

When sailing in the dark on any course, a difficulty is that the awkward wave cannot be seen until it is right on top of the yacht. With experience it is possible to develop a sixth sense which helps in anticipating the waves to come. Reactions will also be quicker with practice and enable a surprise wave to be parried at the last moment. Yet when it is really dark, even the best helmsman will tend to give the watch on deck a wetter ride, and those below will get more shaken about. Conversely the coming of dawn normally brings the feeling that the seas have moderated.

9.1 Watch the seas to windward and ahead. When a steep breaking wave threatens to strike, keep up speed, then luff nearly head to wind. As the bow breaks through, heave up the helm to bear away as the wave passes under the hull.

Sailing to windward

Trouble may come from sailing fast into the face of a steep wave, especially when it happens to come from more ahead than the general run of the waves. Her speed will drive the bows to dig into such a wave and the deck may be swept by a few tons of water determined to show its power. Speed can also cause the yacht to take off from the crest of a wave and land in the trough with a mighty thump which shakes everything on board in extreme cases.

The helmsman begins to manoeuvre the boat as it sails down the back of the wave preceding the awkward one. He turns towards the wind until the sail lifts to ease the speed of the boat, which then climbs the wave almost head on. Ideally, she should have no more than the minimum steerage way when she reaches the crest of the wave; then she should be steered off the wind to gain speed once more.

The practised rough weather helmsman will weave a course among the waves without conscious thought, keeping the boat relatively dry and the motion moderate.

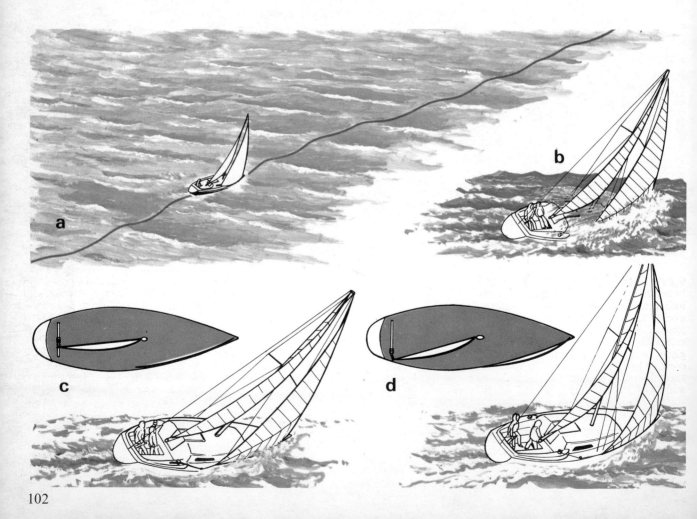

9.2 a) The helmsman must weave a course between as many waves as possible, only luffing to meet a big one that he cannot avoid, and then immediately bearing away on the crest. **b)** If he fails to luff the wave will break against the side forward, giving a severe shake-up to boat and crew. **c)** In really steep seas it is wrong to sheet the sails in flat and the traveller amidships. **d)** It is better to ease sheets slightly to give enough speed and acceleration to give certain steering.

9.3 Too much speed sometimes results in the boat leaping through a crest and crashing into the back of the next wave ahead. A racing crew will have a very alert and experienced helmsman in these conditions who will use all his strength to ease the slamming and to force the boat to conform to the fastest course. When cruising this is quite out of the question and so speed must be reduced.

Tacking

a

b

Gybing

d

c

9.4 When tacking in a big sea, it is essential to keep up the speed just before the tack and to have a second person to handle the headsail sheets. As the yacht breaks through the crest of a wave, push the helm over firmly and ease the mainsheet (or let it go altogether if necessary). Hold the jib back momentarily (**a**), and then let it go. The boat should be kept well free on the new tack (**b**) while the sheets are winched in and speed picks up.

Gybing at **c**, needs careful control of the mainsail. Sheet it in nearly amidships before the gybe and then wait until the boat is travelling fast down the face of a wave, when the pressure will ease. In this way there is less risk of a 'chinese' gybe (**d**) and broken battens. There is also less risk to the crew.

Beam seas

When the course puts the seas on the beam she will be easier to steer so long as the sails are properly trimmed. In moderate conditions she will normally ride comfortably if steered away from the occasional big wave, so as to take it on the quarter. Once she is almost on the crest she should be steered round to her course again.

Should the seas become really rough, the swirl in her wake as she turns away leaves a slick that can cause a steep wave to break over her. In these conditions it may be better to turn towards the big wave, just as when sailing to windward. The manoeuvre needs to start sooner and be not too fast, because there is much further to luff, and centrifugal force may cause excessive heeling.

There may come a time when the waves are too short and steep to allow the yacht to turn either away from or towards them. The warning of a wave top filling the cockpit will mean that she must give up sailing her chosen course, and adopt one of the alternatives described in the following pages.

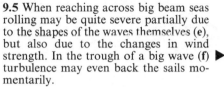

9.5 When reaching across big beam seas rolling may be quite severe partially due to the shapes of the waves themselves (e), but also due to the changes in wind strength. In the trough of a big wave (f) turbulence may even back the sails momentarily.

9.6 Careful steering is needed in beam seas. The main danger is a big breaking wave close to the yacht. The helmsman should bear away and run before a big breaker (g), luffing again as the crest passes beneath the yacht. If the waves are big enough it will neither be safe to bear away, nor to luff up. The final warning is a cascade of water sweeping across the decks, filling the cockpit and perhaps even flooding the cabin. When this happens something further has to be done such as heaving-to or running before the seas.

Following seas

With the wind and seas astern the yacht will continue to ride with reasonable comfort, when she would be thoroughly wet and uncomfortable sailing to windward. Yet in some ways her steering will need more experience as the warnings of the sea building up are less obvious. An experienced helmsman will often be quite happy wearing light weather clothes in a very strong following wind with no water coming aboard, while an inexperienced helmsman would certainly not have such good control in these conditions, and any slip in steering could make the cockpit thoroughly wet and even endanger someone not secured by a safety harness.

9.7 Running before a big sea the decks are dry, but it would be quite different if the helmsman lost concentration.

9.8 The secret of good steering downwind is anticipation. Once a lurch, roll, or broach has started, it is liable to throw the helmsman off balance and, in regaining his position, he momentarily eases the helm just at the time greatest pressure is needed. In the extreme positions (**a** and **b**) it is very difficult indeed to apply full helm owing to the helmsman's body weight actually hindering his effort, and because his position in the cockpit is uncomfort-

Anticipation when steering

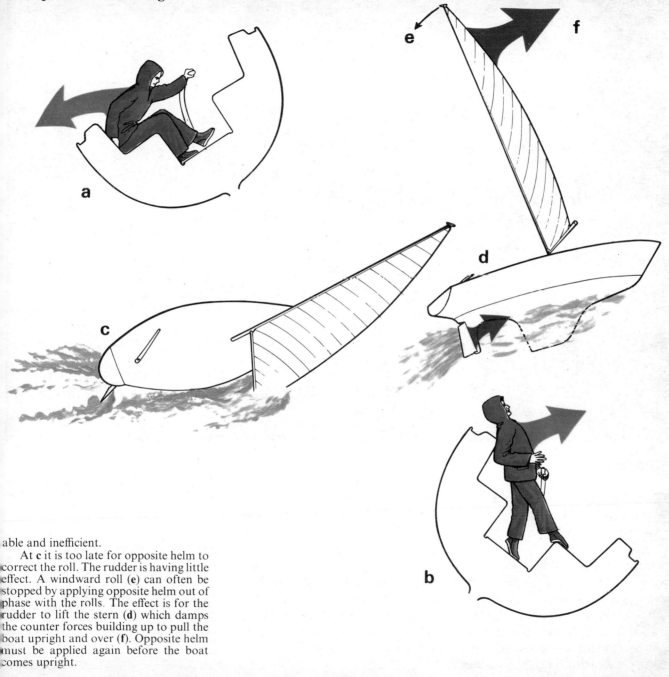

able and inefficient.

At **c** it is too late for opposite helm to correct the roll. The rudder is having little effect. A windward roll (**e**) can often be stopped by applying opposite helm out of phase with the rolls. The effect is for the rudder to lift the stern (**d**) which damps the counter forces building up to pull the boat upright and over (**f**). Opposite helm must be applied again before the boat comes upright.

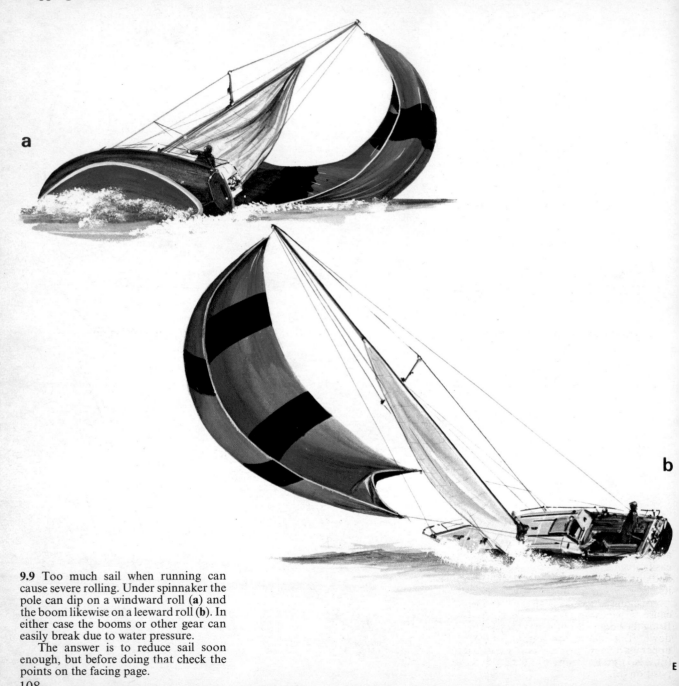

9.9 Too much sail when running can cause severe rolling. Under spinnaker the pole can dip on a windward roll (**a**) and the boom likewise on a leeward roll (**b**). In either case the booms or other gear can easily break due to water pressure.

The answer is to reduce sail soon enough, but before doing that check the points on the facing page.

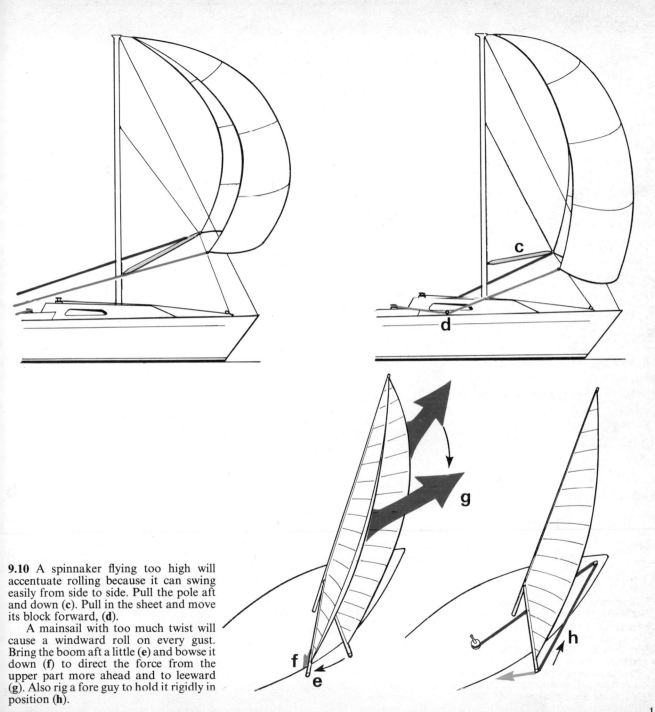

9.10 A spinnaker flying too high will accentuate rolling because it can swing easily from side to side. Pull the pole aft and down (**c**). Pull in the sheet and move its block forward, (**d**).

A mainsail with too much twist will cause a windward roll on every gust. Bring the boom aft a little (**e**) and bowse it down (**f**) to direct the force from the upper part more ahead and to leeward (**g**). Also rig a fore guy to hold it rigidly in position (**h**).

Reefing and reducing sail

Means of reducing sail are:
—Lowering a sail altogether
—Changing a sail for a smaller one
—Reefing to reduce the sail area

Lowering any sail will have the effect of reducing power. With a two-masted rig the mizzen can be lowered to reduce sail without the need for anyone to go forward. Alternatively, the mainsail can be dropped with the boat still under control sailing with a small jib and mizzen. A single-masted boat will tend to be unbalanced if one sail is lowered, and may be unable to tack in a rough sea, but some boats sail quite well under headsail alone. Sail changes normally start with shifting the genoa for a progressively smaller headsail.

Cruising yachts should always be fitted with mainsails that will reef in some way, while sometimes headsails can be reefed as well. Reefing also lowers the centre of effort and thus the heeling moment.

When sailing to windward there is plenty of encouragement to reduce sail in plenty of time; but when running before a rising wind the crew could well be misled into not appreciating how difficult it will be for a light crew to reduce sail on turning onto the wind. The relative wind speed across the deck then becomes much stronger, and may even double in velocity and the motion will also be much more violent.

Should there be the need to reduce sail rapidly, the quickest way with a single-masted rig is to tack, keeping the headsail sheet turned up, and then let go the headsail halyard. The foot of the sail will be held taut on the windward side, keeping the sail partly under control, and the half lowered sail will act as a brake to slow the boat down. The man at the halyard can then move forward more safely from the relative haven of the mast, to haul down and secure the rest of the sail.

The foredeck is generally the wettest and most lively part of the boat, so jobs there should be completed before it gets too rough, especially in the dark. In worsening weather this means changing in good time to the smallest headsail likely to be needed when the wind reaches its maximum. Work around the mast, especially when hove-to, is drier and safer than right forward, so reefing the mainsail can come later. This will be quite easy in the hove-to situation as the luff of the sail is then under very little strain.

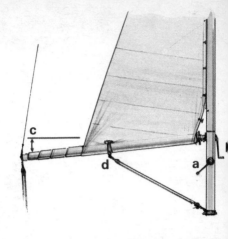

9.11 (top) Roller reefing is the simplest and, provided the gear is maintained, is the most trouble free. One man can operate both the halyard (**a**) and the roller gear (**b**).

9.12 (bottom) The reef point system. The tack (**e**) and the clew (**f**) have to be lashed down in turn, and then all the reef points (**g**).

9.13 (right) Jiffy reefing is the best compromise for racing boats. One man can ease the halyard and hook on the new tack (**h**). Then he can pull out the clew tackle (**j**).

9.14 Points to note when reefing:

1. In roller reefing (9.11) the boom end may drop (**c**). Claw-rings have to be used for attachments along the boom (**d**).

2. With the reef point system, tie the points under the sail only and not under the boom as well. This reef does not interfere with boom fittings.

3. Jiffy reefing is nearly as quick as the roller method and the sail sets well. The bunch at the foot (**k**) can be furled at leisure with a pendant passed through the cringles and over hooks on the boom (**m**).

4. With the last two systems one can lash the boom to the lee rail to steady it in really difficult conditions (left). With all reefs the bottom batten ought to be horizontal to avoid having to take it out.

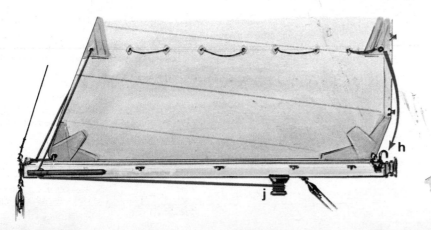

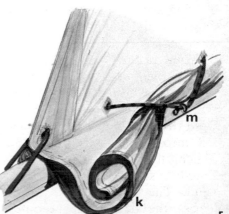

Heaving-to

A boat can be hove-to in the minimum of time, and with no crew effort required beyond the helmsman. The easiest method is simply to tack, leaving the headsail sheet set up. On becoming backed the headsail acts as an effective brake. Meantime the main sheet is eased out as necessary to reduce the drive of the mainsail. It will lift, but it should not be eased so much that it flaps violently.

With the boat sailing close-hauled, all that the helmsman needs to do is to throw over the tiller and ease out the mainsheet. If reaching or running free when the decision is made to heave-to, it is best to haul the headsail sheet taut before tacking, as it will then be much easier than after tacking.

There is some advantage in heaving-to on the starboard tack, as this will give right-of-way over all other craft. If the boat is already sailing on a starboard tack she can be hove-to on the same tack by heaving in on the weather headsail sheet, while easing out on the lee sheet. But this will take longer and will need far more work than simply tacking.

Whichever way it is done, once hove-to the motion of the boat becomes easier and she will heel over less. She will scarcely move ahead through the water yet her sails will steady her. She needs no helmsman, and once settled down all that is needed is an occasional look out from the hatch. She will drift to leeward at about 70 degrees to the direction in which she points.

The amount of drift will depend on the strength of the wind and the shape of the boat, particularly her draft. For instance, in a genuine force 8 gale a shallow draft twin-keeled craft might make a good two knots, while a deep draft boat would make less.

If sea room is limited, with land or a shoal not too far away, then the main sheet and tiller can be adjusted so that the boat makes quiet headway and less leeway. She can be tacked by letting the backed headsail draw until she gains enough speed to be put about on to the other tack. Then she can be hove-to on the new tack.

Lying a-hull

Winds of storm force will be too strong even for heavily reefed sails to remain set. With all sails lowered the boat is said to be lying a-hull, sometimes also called hulling.

With the tiller secured to leeward, a yacht will normally lie almost broadside on to the wind and sea, presenting the greatest buoyancy to the approaching wave; there will be least chance of damage to the rudder if she is thrown bodily to leeward.

She will roll more heavily than when hove-to and, in a steep sea rolling can become so violent as to be thoroughly uncomfortable down below. Gear needs to be particularly well secured or wedged in place to prevent any breaking adrift; a cooking pot hurtling across a cabin could give someone in the lee bunk a nasty crack.

A boat lying a-hull will make leeway depending upon her draft and the windage of her hull and top hamper. Taking the mainsail off its boom and stowing it below will reduce windage and cut down drift. In a full force 8 gale a shallow draft boat with normal top hamper should allow that she might drift as much as ten miles in a four hour blow. She would also move ahead as much as four miles in the same time, because the hull and coachroof act like a sail.

9.15 Heaving-to is a rough weather technique that can also be used for any temporary stop or for the purpose of lowering a headsail when short handed. When close hauled or close reaching (a), it can be accomplished instantly by tacking without letting go the old lee sheet (b). The backed headsail brakes the yacht. The mainsail is adjusted until the boat makes practically no headway and lies comfortably; the helm is then lashed a-lee.

A boat lying a-hull will roll heavily and uncomfortably (c). If the seas become very steep a wave could break over her. The addition of a small amount of sail can reduce rolling (d).

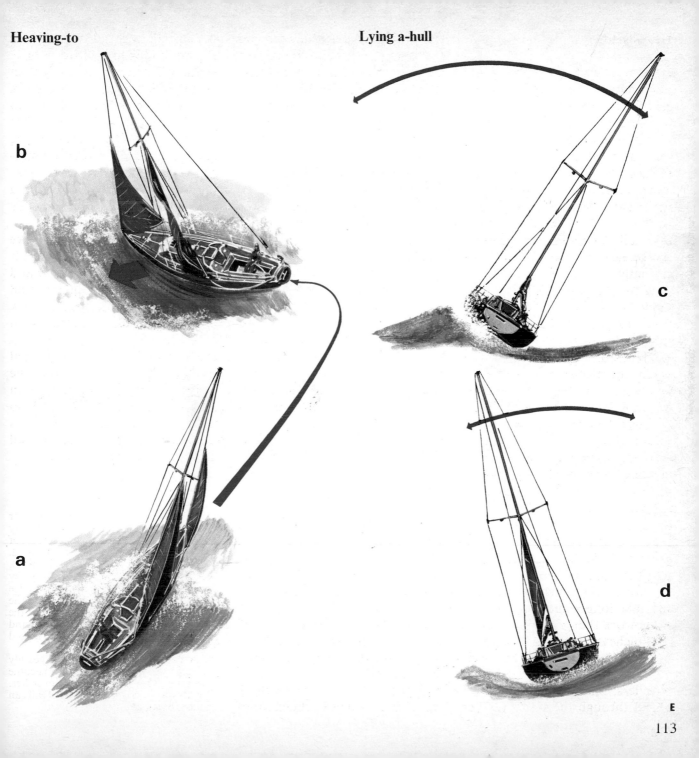

Heaving-to

Lying a-hull

b

c

a

d

9.16 This dramatic photo was taken from a lifeboat towing warps in heavy seas. The loop of rope can be seen on the front surface of the wave and one part is just starting to induce a break in that part of the crest.

9.17 The best effect is obtained by towing a long warp in a bight with a canvas bucket at the apex.

E

Running under bare poles

A really heavy breaking sea can be dangerous to a small craft lying a-hull when the breaking tops of the waves are higher than her freeboard. Such a weight of water may crash down upon her cabin top and deck as to cause actual structural damage. To avoid this the yacht can be steered off to run before the waves under bare poles. A typical 30 ft. deep-draft sloop, with her mainsail carefully stowed on its boom and other sails stowed down below, was logged as driving at four knots before a gale force 8.

Had the lowering of the mainsail been delayed until a neat stow was impracticable, and a headsail had been left lashed on deck, she would have gone faster than this. Thus ample sea room to leeward is essential as even a four hour gale could drive her twenty miles to leeward under bare poles. Even in this state the yacht will almost certainly need to be steered to prevent broaching. The technique is to point the stern at each big wave as it rolls up behind her.

9.18 One end should be led to a winch to ease the work when the time comes to recover the warp.

Towing warps

Even under bare poles there is a risk of broaching which will be lessened if she can be slowed down still more. Speed can be reduced by trailing ropes over the stern; the best result comes from the longest and biggest rope available, trailed in a bight, with a canvas bucket secured to the bight and with the two ends made fast on each side of the yacht right aft. This has the effect of steadying the boat, so that she becomes easier to steer.

Another beneficial effect of this method is that the ropes form a slick in the sea well back from the boat. This will encourage a wave to break clear astern instead of right over the cockpit.

Once the boat has steadied down with ropes trailed astern, it becomes easier to leave the cockpit and work on deck. Thus the sails can then be re-secured to reduce windage, while anything loosened by severe rolling when lying a-hull can be attended to.

Lying to a sea anchor

The sea anchor, or drogue, has been used in certain types of craft for lying to a gale, but for the conventionally shaped cruising yachts a sea anchor needs to be very large to have much effect. Thus it is seldom carried about a small yacht.

Its use would be very limited as, when streamed out from right forward the boat will normally lie with her stern still pointing partially towards the seas. This is due to her short keel coupled with the windage of her mast and rigging. A long-keeled ship's lifeboat, on the other hand, with no mast stepped, will lie to a sea anchor almost heading into the seas.

Used by the cruising yacht, her drift will be scarcely less than when lying a-hull, and her motion no less violent.

Indeed there have been reports of yachts in very bad weather becoming less uncomfortable after the sea anchor broke adrift.

Anchoring at sea

A yacht has few options left open should she be caught off a lee shore in a gale when unable to sail windward. This could be due to some damage, or because the gale was too strong for her, even with the aid of the engine. The problem

9.19 Lying a-hull, the windage of topsides and rig together is further forward than the centre of lateral resistance of the underwater profile (upper, right). Hence the modern yacht tends to lie pointing to leeward. Even a massive sea anchor will not pull her head to wind and may cause damage by preventing the hull from giving to the seas. The long-keeled lifeboat, on the other hand, is more likely to lie heading into seas (lower right).

A drogue (**a**) should have a strong attachment with a swivel (**b**) and a tripping line (**c**).

of reducing drift to leeward is then acute.

Her most vital equipment in such a situation is a good anchor with ample chain cable. In water too deep for the anchor to reach the bottom it will still check her drift to leeward. Then as the bottom shoals when the yacht approaches the coast or some offlying hazard, the anchor will reach the bottom; assuming a reasonable length of cable and

gradual shoaling, this should be some time before the shallow water effect starts to build up the waves. However, if the coast is steep-to, the situation may be very serious since, not only will the boat be close in, but the effects of reflected waves from the cliffs will cause a severely turbulent sea.

However, let us hope for the best; at first the anchor may only reduce the speed of drift but as the depth lessens it may get a good

grip and hold.

This will still be a truly unhappy position, but yachts have safely ridden at anchor through a gale at sea. At least the anchor will buy vital time, during which the wind may shift or moderate, the tide may turn, or repairs can be completed so that she can claw out to seawards.

It may also give time for help to come. Certainly it is a situation when a distress call is justified.

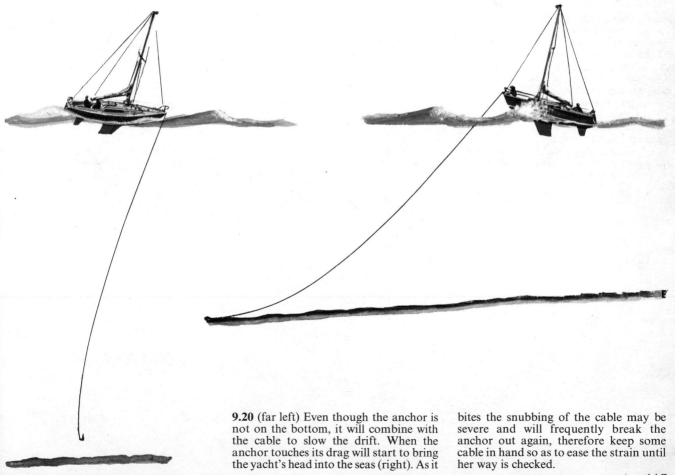

9.20 (far left) Even though the anchor is not on the bottom, it will combine with the cable to slow the drift. When the anchor touches its drag will start to bring the yacht's head into the seas (right). As it bites the snubbing of the cable may be severe and will frequently break the anchor out again, therefore keep some cable in hand so as to ease the strain until her way is checked.

Oil in troubled waters

Traditionally oil is poured on troubled waters to quieten them. Indeed a very small quantity of the right oil in the right place has an amazing ability to smooth the seas, and in particular to discourage the big wave from breaking in the open sea. It is less effective in a tide race or for waves breaking in shallow water.

Fish oil is usually considered the best, but yachts are unlikely to carry more of this than the few spoonfuls in a sardine tin. Engine lubricating oil is quite effective, the heavier the better, but paraffin, or kerosene, which some yachts use for cooking, is very little use.

Oil takes time to spread and if the boat is moving at any speed the oil is left astern too quickly to give any benefit. When the boat is almost stationary, such as when

9.21 Close in to a lee shore the waves may become very steep and the foredeck may become untenable. The anchor will tend to keep her heading into the waves even if it drags. The heavier the cable the less will be the snubbing when it does finally bite.

E

hove-to or lying a-hull, oil can be thoroughly effective if it can be made to spread over the sea surface to windward of her.

Traditionally a canvas oil bag is used, pierced by a few holes with a marline spike. Such bags are unlikely to be to hand in a small yacht today although sometimes seen in Norwegian chandleries, but spare lubricating oil will normally be carried in the convenient cans in which it is bought. Such cans will serve well, with two or three small holes made by a spike.

The can needs to be firmly secured, with a rope right round it as well as through the handle, and then trailed over the side. It should be secured well forward to prevent it hitting someone in the cockpit if hurled back on board by a wave. If the can is thrown back amidships before its oil has become effective it will make the deck slippery and the ropes difficult to handle, so try to avoid this happening too.

Another method is to pump oil out through the head, or ship's lavatory; a tablespoonful every few minutes is about the dose if the boat is moving really slowly. However, this method is seldom popular with the crew of a cruising yacht not feeling too well, as crouching alongside the head in an oily atmosphere can lead to seasickness.

9.22 Oil has an amazing ability to smooth rough seas and the slick from a couple of small holes pierced in a can of lubricating oil can last long enough for repairs to be made or gear re-secured. Specially made oil bags can also be used, or the oil pumped out via the heads or ship's lavatory.

10 Man overboard!

In any weather conditions a man overboard is serious, but in rough weather it is truly dangerous.

Rough or calm the same immediate action is required; this should be so well known to each member of the crew that it can be done spontaneously, even if it is dark and rough, with seasickness aboard. Correct response will depend upon frequent practice under easier conditions.

The first essential is to throw overboard the life buoy, which can be done by whoever is nearest to it; usually this is the helmsman, as the life buoy should be placed within easy reach of the steering position when at sea.

At the same time the thrower must let out a shout of 'Man Overboard', loud enough for everyone below to hear, even if asleep.

The next step is for the helmsman to steady the boat on her previous course. This enables personal bearings to be regained, as an accident of this sort, followed by violent action to throw over the life buoy, may leave him confused, uncertain of the direction of the wind, or the man in the water.

It is sound practice to count five after dropping the life buoy and alerting the crew. This allows time for a reasoned judgement on the best plan for recovery, whether the crew left on board is just yourself or includes others struggling up from below.

This is a top emergency which allows no time to don deck clothing; survival of the man overboard demands absolute urgency. The job of the first person to join the helmsman must be to keep his eyes firmly fixed on the man in the water.

10.2 It is one person's sole task to keep the swimmer in sight however the boat manoeuvres.

Immediate action—check these points:	
Throw the life buoy	From its ready-use stowage near the helmsman, together with its light and line, if fitted (photo, left).
Shout 'Man Overboard'	Loud enough to wake a sleeping crew.
Steady on course	Turn back to original course.
Count five and think	Steady oneself and plan the next action.
Call up the crew	First person on deck keeps watch on the man in the water.

10.1

Regaining contact

Unlike the first stage, for which actions should be automatic, the second stage to regain contact needs, in rough weather, a considered decision as to what is best suited to the conditions of weather and crew. Possible methods under sail are:

— To gybe round back to the man
— To tack back to the man
— To reach away until ready and then reach back

The classic man overboard manoeuvre under sail is to gybe, carrying on round until the boat stops head to wind beside the man.

Yet this manoeuvre depends on no hang ups from the sheets, guys, topping lift or sails, besides perfect judgement in rough conditions. Should any of these go wrong, the man's situation is much more dangerous. Therefore the gybing method is likely to be best when the boat is sailing to windward, and conditions are such that no hitch is likely to arise from a hurried gybe.

In bad conditions, and with the crew one short, a gybe might split the mainsail or cause other damage to disable the yacht in some way, then it might be better to tack. Yet if the boat is sailing on the wind, or even reaching, an immediate tack will bring her to windward of the man, so she will

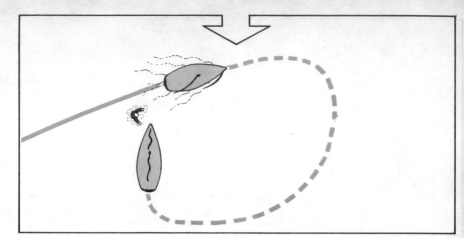

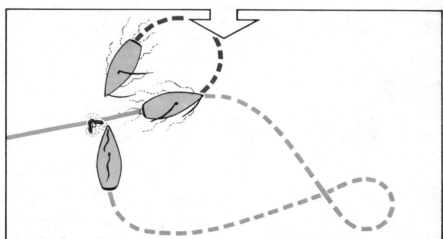

10.3 (Upper) The classic method involving an immediate gybe which works in quiet weather when everything is handled correctly.

10.4 (Lower) The boat can also be tacked after first running off (light blue track). An immediate tack (dark blue) would bring the boat running past the man too fast for recovery.

have to turn down wind to reach him. He could be missed altogether due to the speed, but even if the boat happens to sail close past him, she will be going much too fast for him to catch and secure a rope without damaging himself.

Therefore, if the decision is made to turn back by tacking, the

boat must first run off until she is somewhat to leeward of him, so that when she tacks the boat is able to luff up beside him head to wind. There is then far more accurate control than when running down at him so that positioning can be more accurate. Then also it is easier to judge

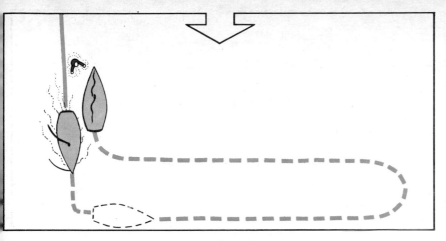

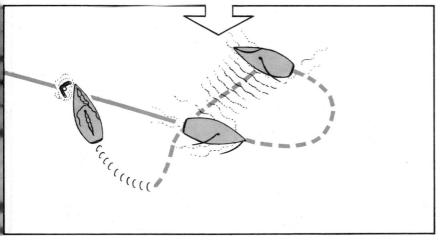

10.5 (Upper) When running turn beam on to the wind. Then, under careful control, sail a beam reach, tack and return on the reciprocal course.

10.6 (Lower) When short-handed or handicapped by gear failure, tack and heave-to, then start the engine and lower sails.

when to turn into the wind to stop the boat.

Running before the wind in rough weather it is likely that a main boom fore-guy will have been rigged. Even without this it will take some time for the watch below to come on deck to trim the sheets. An effective plan under

these conditions is to turn the boat to bring the wind on the beam, calling for one of the crew to note the exact time and, when a log is fitted, the distance.

Meantime, the boat is prepared for tacking, and, when ready, the time and log are again noted, then the boat is put about to bring the

wind abeam on the other side. The time taken and the distance on the log since first turning can therefore be calculated by simple subtraction. When the boat has sailed back the same distance, or for the same time, then the man should be close to windward, so the boat can be turned head to wind to stop beside him.

It may happen that the boat's ability to manoeuvre under sail is limited; this could be due to some accident which also caused the man to fall overboard, for instance the parting of a main sheet or halyard. The decision might then be made to regain contact with the man using the engine alone.

The boat should tack to the heave-to position, keeping the weather headsail sheet set up. Next the engine is started, but kept out of gear until sails are stowed and a check made that nothing is over the side which could foul the propeller.

With no need for a helmsman before moving ahead again, all hands can quickly lower and stow the sails, ensuring that a gust of wind cannot get hold of part of a sail to make the boat uncontrollable under power. Next should be a final check that there is nothing over the side, and then the engine clutch can be engaged to move towards the man. If the boat was hove-to quickly and sails stowed smartly, she will never have got far from the man, who may even have swum near the boat.

A moving propeller is a real danger to anyone in the water, so, once the man has secured a line thrown to him, it is best to stop the engine in case the gear lever should be accidentally engaged.

In rough weather particularly, the final approach to a man overboard is best made approximately head to wind so that the boat is nearly stopped. The man then has the best chance of getting a good hold on a rope thrown to him; if possible he should secure it to his safety harness, if worn, or with a bowline round his waist. If it is unlikely that he can tie a bowline, or has no harness, throw the line with the bowline already tied so that he can slip it over his head and shoulders.

Should he be unable to hold on to or secure the line, it may be necessary for a good swimmer to go to him on the end of another line so that together they can be hauled back alongside the boat.

Getting him aboard

Even when firmly secured close alongside the boat, there may still be a difficult task to get him safely aboard. Anyone in complete rough weather sailing clothes is amazingly heavy as soon as lifted clear of the seas. If he is cold, shocked, or perhaps injured, he will be able to do little to help

himself. However, should he be unhurt and still be feeling strong, then steps can quickly be formed alongside the boat from a couple of bights of rope such as the headsail sheet; one should be just below the surface and one a little higher.

The man will certainly need help to haul himself clear of the water, but if he can stand up in the bottom rope step for about a minute, much of the water will run out of his clothing and make him lighter for the next move.

Better than the bights of rope is a boarding ladder, if one is carried on board. It needs to be firmly secured in place, as in rough weather it could otherwise come adrift as soon as someone got hold of it.

When the casualty is injured or too exhausted to make any effort, the old-established method is to lower a bight of the mainsail into the water, work the man into it, then hoist the head of the sail until he can be bundled onto the deck.

However, in rough weather with a light crew left on board, it may be important to keep the mainsail hoisted so that the boat remains as steady as possible and hove-to. In this situation part of a spare sail, perhaps a genoa if the jib is set, is hanked along the lower guardrail wire and lashed at each end. A spare halyard, or the topping lift, is then secured to the clew. Again the bight of the sail is

draped over the side into the sea and the man worked into it. The sail is then hoisted until the casualty can be easily handled from the deck.

10.7 Various methods of getting a man back aboard a yacht at sea:

a) Make a double bight out of some rope so that the man can use it as a ladder. He will need help since the rope loops are not very stable.

b) A boarding ladder is excellent but should be well secured. Also, release the lower guard wire to help him get aboard. This is useful for all methods.

c) A weak or unconscious man can be heaved aboard by his armpits when facing outboard. A line secured to his safety harness can help.

d) This method is particularly valuable in rough weather when the crew left on board lacks strength. With the boat hove-to, hank a headsail to the guard rail and put a spare halyard on the clew. Then float him into the bight and hoist him out in the sail with the halyard winch.

a

b

c

d

11 When help is needed

Any vessel receiving a distress signal is bound by law to go to the assistance of the sender unless some other vessel is already doing so. Thus it is imperative that it is used only when there is genuine distress affecting the safety of the craft or those aboard her.

So what is 'genuine distress'? A yacht which misses the tide, when her owner has an appointment ashore and her engine will not start is not in distress, whatever the feelings of her owner. If his boat shows a red flare, he is committing an offence for which he can be held personally responsible. Indeed he might be liable to pay compensation for the expense occurred in answering a call; this could be heavy if the answering ship happens to be a liner with a schedule to keep.

Yet a yacht with all her crew so seasick as to be incapable of working their craft could be in genuine distress if the yacht is drifting towards a lee shore or a dangerous race.

Distress signals

Signals which can be most readily used by a small yacht in distress during rough weather include:
—'MAYDAY' on the radio telephone
—Red flares
—Orange coloured smoke
—Flames and smoke, such as from burning oil-soaked rags
—SOS ($\cdots$ – – – $\cdots$) flashed by torch or heliograph
—International code flags NC
—Ensign hoisted upside down
—A square flag with a ball above or below it
—Continuous sounding, or SOS, on any fog signal apparatus
—Any unfamiliar shape, such as a torn sail or a blanket, hoisted on the mast
—Outstretched arms raised and lowered slowly.

Some of these are not international distress signals, but may attract attention so that binoculars are focused on the craft. It should then be quite easy to establish that she is in distress. There are other generally recognised signals to attract attention when *not* in distress, such as the showing of white flares.

Radio telephone

Radio telephones, when fitted in a yacht, should normally be used only by those qualified to operate them. However, everyone on board should be able to send a distress call should the operator be disabled. The international distress frequency is 2182 kHz, and all merchant ships listen on this wavelength on 'standby'. Very few small yachts have a transmitter with 2182 kHz facilities, most having only a VHF set. If the latter, in some countries one can call the local coastal station on Channel 16 and ask to be connected to the Coastguard. Coastguards themselves, and other small boats too, will possibly be listening and pick up your message direct. The disadvantage is that your range is very short, not much more than visual. In the U.S., local coastal stations do not monitor Channel 16; the range of the Coast Guard VHF system is, however, considerable, and commercial ships monitor 16 everywhere.

There are also other types of special distress transmitters. Some are automatic, some can also be made to transmit a personal morse message, and some can also receive. They operate on

a variety of frequencies depending on type, some on 2182 kHz, some on the military frequency of 500 kHz, and some on special aircraft frequencies. Helicopters use only VHF or UHF and can work Channel 16. So after tuning to the right frequency and switching on, the exact procedure should be used which is as follows:
— 'MAYDAY MAYDAY MAYDAY' (the internationally recognised distress code word)
— 'This is yacht SUNSHINE SUNSHINE SUNSHINE' (or whatever the yacht's name is, said three times)
— 'MAYDAY SUNSHINE'
— 'Position off the Owers' (or wherever the yacht is believed to be)
— 'Taking in water fast' (or whatever is the nature of the distress)
— 'Require immediate help' (or whatever aid is required)
— 'Over'

11.1 Any vessel has a legal obligation to help another in distress, but can make a salvage claim for property saved.

There should be a reply from anyone hearing the message, but if none comes, check that the set is correctly switched on and tuned. Then repeat the whole procedure. Once a reply has been heard and communications are established, further information should be sent, starting each message with the word 'MAYDAY'.

The most vital information for such a rescue is the position of the yacht in trouble. Even professional seafarers have at times seriously hindered rescue by reporting an incorrect position, while a small craft in rough weather may well be far away from her believed position. Thus it is important not to give an impression of accuracy which is not justified.

When uncertain of the position, a valuable clue to the rescue organization is to name the place and time from which she sailed and to quote her intended destination. It would be even further help to state, for example, that a light flashing brightly in groups of three about every twenty seconds was bearing about north. This would be better than guessing the identity of the light, and perhaps giving the wrong one.

Visual distress signals

The most important visual signals are pyrotechnics specially designed for the purpose, but it is important to make the best use of them.

The most powerful type for small craft is the hand-held parachute rocket. This shoots a red flare up to as much as 1,000 feet, which then burns brilliantly for half a minute as it slowly descends. On a clear dark night parachute flares may be visible more than ten miles away, yet in bad weather the visibility will be very much less. Should there be low cloud the flare may waste its brilliance and burn out before it gets down to the cloud base, but in this case it can be fired at an angle to get less height.

Star signals are effective in attracting attention at a reasonable distance. They are held in the hand and when ignited shoot into the air a succession of red stars, each burning for about five seconds. Meantime the flare itself continues to burn with a bright red light for about three quarters of a minute.

Simple hand flares burn with a bright red light for about one minute. They are usually as bright as the parachute flares, but as they burn only a few feet above the sea surface, their visibility is limited both by the curvature of the earth and the height of the waves.

During the minute that the flare is burning it is unlikely that both craft would simultaneously be on the crest of waves for more than a second or two. So if the waves are only six feet high it is probable that even at two miles the flare would not attract attention. The higher it is held, therefore, the better.

Flag signals will usually go unnoticed as those carried by a yacht are so small. However a torn sail or any unfamiliar shape hoisted by a yacht will attract attention and once a ship has binoculars trained on a craft it is easy to show her distress.

Life saving craft

Craft specially designed for saving life at sea operate in most coastal waters. Some are state maintained, such as the U.S. Coast Guards; others are maintained by private organizations such as the Royal National Lifeboat Institution, which operates around the coasts of England and Wales, Scotland and Ireland. In each case the craft are particularly suited to the area; their crews, whether professional or amateur, are experts with great knowledge of those waters.

The U.S. Coast Guards operate both air and surface craft; the Royal National Lifeboat Institution, on the other hand, operates lifeboats which work in close co-operation with the state con-

11.2 In this case the flames from the burning yacht will provide a continuing beacon, but in all cases it is wise to take an immediate bearing. It might have been their last flare!

trolled Coastguards, and aircraft from the Royal Air Force and the Royal Navy, usually helicopters.

It matters little to a boat in distress who operates the rescue craft, so long as it comes quickly and knows its job. In most countries there is an efficient rescue organization to see that a distress call is answered as quickly as possible. In bad weather coastguards keep watch and, as soon as a distress signal is received, will set the rescue organization into motion. Sometimes this actually happens before those aboard the craft themselves realize that they are in trouble, and a lifeboat will be launched to stand by a craft seen to be in a dangerous situation.

Lifeboats in some areas show a blue flashing light to indicate their identity but they are nearly always distinctive in appearance. Yachtsmen should appreciate that the coxswain of such craft are very experienced seamen, whose opinions should weigh heavily in the decisions a yacht's skipper must make. Lifeboats exist primarily for saving life, so it can be accepted with confidence that any advice given will be based on this.

Lifeboats offer their services in saving lives freely, although those run by voluntary subscriptions welcome any contribution towards their funds by those grateful for rescue. A lifeboat crew, when life is no longer at risk and no other craft is in distress, may offer to tow a yacht into safety, and lifeboats are particularly well suited to do this (*11.1*).

In such cases a lifeboatman has the legal right of any seaman to claim a reward for salvage. Such claims are rare, as this service is normally given voluntarily and the Royal National Lifeboat Institution itself never claims salvage. Yet should such a claim be made by the crew on their own behalf, it would be awarded by a court only when the salvors could prove that it was fully justified.

Once a distress signal has been answered it is best to reserve the remaining flares until a search craft is in the area. Lifeboats are often equipped with radio telephones, so if direct communication can be established, the lifeboat will ask for signals to be fired when it is somewhere near the casualty.

Should it be decided to abandon the yacht when the lifeboat comes, then preparation should be made. The skipper should check that everyone has a lifejacket correctly in position, and all should know what has been planned. Abandoning the yacht demands rigid discipline, as people can be severely injured should the lifeboat and yacht be thrown together heavily by the seas, and it is particularly dangerous to fall between them. Special care must be taken of anyone who is partly disabled by injury or seasickness.

Lives have been lost in attempting to salvage valuable equipment. Should there be anything particularly important it should be secured in a sailbag with a line attached and placed ready on deck. Yet absolute priority must always be given to saving lives.

If a big ship comes

Even the smallest yacht, if in distress, might find that a very large ship answers her call. The ship's master is bound to assist in saving life, but not in salvaging the craft, so the yacht's skipper must decide clearly what assistance he needs in that a big ship can aid in various different ways, such as:
—Taking off the crew of the yacht
—Transferring a seriously injured person
—Sending medical aid to an injured person
—Giving a lee for the yacht to overcome her own problems
—Standing by and homing special rescue craft to the position.

Taking off the crew in rough weather will normally require that the big ship comes close alongside the yacht to windward, using a boarding ladder. When she gets alongside, the yacht is likely to be heavily battered in spite of all the fenders she has prepared. It will be alarming, noisy and dangerous.

The skipper should previously have made quite clear to all in the yacht that he intends the crew to abandon her; he should also give the order for leaving, preferably selecting someone strong and agile as the first to go up the boarding ladder, and himself leaving only when the others have gone, since he must supervise the whole operation.

The first thing for the yacht when alongside, is to secure lines from the ship so that the yacht remains in the same position fore and aft, with the boarding ladder well clear of the yacht's mast, which may otherwise damage someone climbing up the ladder.

Even on the lee side of the ship the yacht may be moving up and down her side ten feet or more with the roll of the ship. Thus each person in turn must try to get on to the boarding ladder when the yacht is at the top of their relative movement, quickly climbing up clear to avoid being crushed should the yacht ride up any higher.

He must not delay while on the ladder to try to pass up gear for salvage, as absolute priority must be given to the safety of all those in the yacht. Indeed no time should be lost when each person goes up in turn under the direction of the skipper, as the yacht is

11.3 (Above) The ship provides a lee with the apex reaching about one and a quarter times its length to leeward. The yacht will lose the wind in this area and so should be under power. A doctor can be transferred in an inflatable dinghy.

(Below) The yacht must secure lines fore and aft, the ladder must be clear of the mast and the crew must climb fast. The yacht will certainly be damaged and must be abandoned. Code flags NC mean 'I need immediate assistance'.

inevitably in danger when alongside a ship in heavy weather.

Any vital equipment for salvage should previously have been put in a sailbag ready on deck. If the opportunity arises the yacht can call for a further line from the ship, and this can be secured to the bag by someone waiting for his turn to go up the ladder.

On a dark night it is easy enough to get confused over who has been rescued. Thus the skipper must concentrate on seeing that each goes up in his turn and no-one has slipped below for some personal treasure. When the skipper himself goes up the ladder he should be able to report with certainty that all have been rescued.

It must be appreciated that after a small yacht has been alongside a ship in rough seas, she is likely to be severely damaged and quite unable to withstand the strains of being towed by a large ship which would need to steam at perhaps seven or eight knots to have steerage way.

On rescuing the yacht's people, the responsibility of the ship's master to the yacht is at an end. Unless it be a relatively small and manoeuvrable ship he will almost certainly have to abandon the yacht but might report her position by radio so that some more suitable craft could take her in tow if she remains afloat.

Transferring an injured person in rough weather entails the use of another boat if the yacht is not to risk being lost alongside the ship. Best for this is an inflatable dinghy which can bump alongside without squashing anyone or damaging itself.

The inflatable should operate only in the area of lee which normally extends to about one and a quarter lengths of a ship lying broadside on to a moderate gale. The area of lee will itself be moving as the ship drifts to leewards; for instance a 400 ft. long ship drifting at one knot will cross its lee area in about five minutes. A sailing craft coming into this area to slip her dinghy with the injured man will be partly blanketed from the wind, so must be very careful that the ship does not drift down on top of her. In these circumstances the use of an auxiliary is virtually essential.

The dinghy must be specially careful to keep away from the after end of the ship where the pitch may bring the stern crashing down on top of her.

Medical aid to a yacht in distress will probably require the ship to lower a lifeboat to transfer a doctor or medical equipment. Again the yacht should attempt to be in the lee area for the transfer, again taking care that the ship does not drift down on her.

Helicopter pick-up

Helicopters are part of the rescue services in many countries, so a distress call may well be answered by one. It will normally hover above the craft in distress, sometimes lowering one of its crew on a wire and then winching up those needing rescue.

The pick-up can be direct from the deck of a boat without a mast, but it would be too dangerous from a sailing yacht whose mast is cavorting through the air and liable to foul the helicopter pick-up wire. In these conditions it is best to let out the yacht's inflatable dinghy or liferaft on the end of a long rope and the pick-up can be made from this. If no dinghy or raft is available then each person to be rescued should float out clear of the yacht towards the helicopter rescue man who will already be in the water.

The normal method of pick-up is by a strop passed around the back and chest; with this in place the rescue man will often be winched up with the casualty to steady him.

Should someone be injured in a way that precludes the use of the strop, then the rescue man will come down with a stretcher and strap the casualty firmly into this for winching up to safety or, if this is also impossible, there is a type of net scoop which can lift a man direct out of the sea.

11.4 Helicopters carry a special strop for lifting people. Sometimes a rescue man is lowered and hoisted each time as well, to aid the pick-up.

11.5 A special stretcher is lowered ▶ and an injured crew member is strapped tightly in before hoisting.

11.6 (Below, right) The yacht's mast is dangerous to the helicopter so the people can only be transferred from a dinghy or direct from the sea.

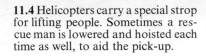

Liferaft

Unless another vessel is standing by, it is best to remain on board a damaged yacht until she is almost certainly sinking, as a yacht is much more visible than a liferaft. However, it may be imperative to use the liferaft without delay.

The first thing to do is to stop the yacht, perhaps by heaving-to. If she is travelling at any speed it will be difficult to secure the liferaft alongside. In a recent case an explosion blew out the cockpit floor, which was followed by flames. The watch on deck were unable to release the genoa sheet and the yacht was still travelling at four or five knots when the liferaft was put overboard. The speed caused the stabiliser drogues to drag in the sea and the liferaft bottom was torn out.

The second action is to secure the liferaft's painter, then release the closures of its container and, if there is room on deck, fire the gas inflator. If space is short, the raft must be put over the side and the gas bottle activated at the same time. The raft should inflate right way up, if not it will have to be righted.

In moderate seas by day, a liferaft sometimes cannot be seen at a distance of only 400 metres; while by night craft searching after previously seeing distress rockets, have been unable to see the raft 200 metres off, even though a torch was being waved from the raft. So it is important to take into the raft all the pyro-technics and waterproof flash-lights available; it is also valuable to take a boathook, from which a daylight distress signal could be waved perhaps two metres above the water.

A pyrotechnic should be used only when there is a good chance of it being sighted; it will be wasted if no ship or land is visible within two or three miles at the most. In a recent case a yacht which was blazing furiously and with the crew in a dinghy nearby firing red parachute rockets, was not seen even though the shore and a lighthouse were clearly visible and other yachts were known to be in the vicinity.

When the time comes to use a flare effectively, firing it should be carefully planned to keep it dry after it is removed from its water-proof container. Also ensure that the remaining pyrotechnics are not accidentally soaked.

On boarding the liferaft, if no other vessel is standing by, the first requirement is to settle down and discover where the emergency equipment is stowed. Cold is likely to be the greatest danger, so it is important to keep the raft as dry as possible.

No-one wants to stay in the liferaft longer than is essential, but it is as well to think of it as a home for the time being and to make it as comfortable as possible. In this way the time before rescue comes can be tolerable instead of being a nightmare. It could be consolation to know that one couple from a sunken yacht were safely rescued after three and a half months in an inflatable raft, which was only designed for a forty-eight hour emergency!

11.7 The liferaft is home for a brief period. Modern yacht rafts are designed to carry 2, 4, 6, 8 or 10 people for about two days, though much longer periods have been recorded.

11.8 Features include the canopy—**a**; double tubes—**b**; CO_2 bottle inflator—**c**; hand or foot pump—**d**; tools, flashlight and knife—**e**; drogue—**f**; emergency food and water (extra water should be taken aboard)—**g**; stabilizer pockets—**h**; insulated floor—**k**; flares—**m**; fishing gear etc.—**n**.

11.9 (Upper, right) The liferaft is contained in a cover which can be flexible or rigid plastic. It must be very firmly secured but has quick-release clips and the raft's painter is permanently secured to the yacht.

11.10 (Lower, right) The painter should always be made fast to a strong point. Quick-release clips sometimes fail to let go in an emergency. Always have the possibility of being able to cut a lashing.

134

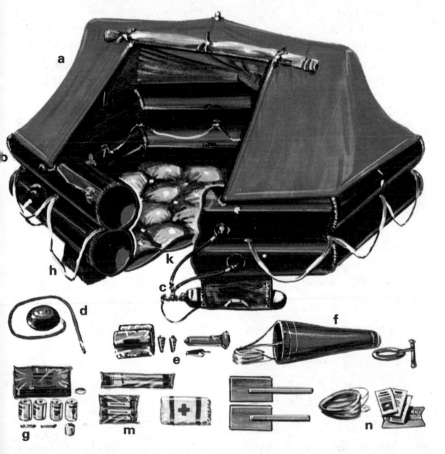

Finally it must be remembered that others can need help too, and it might be your boat that has the duty to provide it. Though the person in charge of a craft receiving a distress signal should not seriously endanger his own craft, her crew or passengers.

There is a limit to what a small boat can do in rough weather; a rescue attempt by an inadequately manned and equipped craft could well make the situation worse for both vessels.

Should it be essential to take off the crew, for instance from a disabled craft drifting onto a dangerous lee shore, only a really experienced skipper with a strong crew should attempt to go close enough for a direct transfer. Otherwise it is safer for all if the transfer is by inflatable dinghy, or by those to be rescued floating well clear of the disabled craft.

Standing by is probably the most valuable service that a small yacht can give to another craft in distress. This greatly increases the chance of a dismasted yacht being located by a vessel better equipped for rescue. Your boat will increase the number of pyrotechnic signals available, and may also be able to act as a radio link both to send a MAYDAY call or to pass instructions and advice.

Perhaps the most important aid of all is the powerful support to morale given by the presence of another craft to those on board the disabled one. Conditions which previously seemed hopeless at once become tolerable. Possibly the crew of the disabled craft will find that another standing by gives all the help they need. The turn of the tide, or passing on of a line squall, may bring about a rapid change of conditions for the better.

END

11.11 If the rescuing yacht cannot get close, a dinghy or lifebelt can be floated down to take the crew off.